The Teacher's Guide to Gifted and Talented Education

The Teacher's Guide to Gifted and Talented Education: Practical Strategies for the Classroom is a guide on ways to build and enhance your understanding of gifted learners with evidence-based hands-on strategies to use in the classroom.

Whether you are looking to improve your own practice or starting out as a Gifted Education coordinator in your school, this book will guide you through each step. Informed by research, and covering essential topics from theoretical frameworks to differentiation and innovative pedagogies, each chapter includes a 'Back to basics' section, which provides the key information for those wanting just enough to get going, a 'Taking it further' section, which offers a more in-depth critique of the content, and a 'Chapter reflection' which provides an opportunity to plan and set goals.

Filled with tips, strategies, checklists, and templates, and written by an author with extensive practical and research experience in the field, this book is an essential resource for all educators, from early childhood through to secondary.

Kate Lafferty is an experienced teacher having worked across primary, secondary, and tertiary sectors for over 24 years as both a generalist teacher and Gifted Education specialist and taught at both under- and post-graduate level at Monash University, University of Melbourne and La Trobe University. She has delivered numerous professional development sessions, and presented at international conferences.

T0383437

The Teacher's Guide to Gifted and Talented Education

Practical Strategies for the Classroom

Kate Lafferty

Routledge
Taylor & Francis Group

LONDON AND NEW YORK

Designed cover image: © Grant Faint/Getty Images

First published 2024
by Routledge
4 Park Square, Milton Park, Abingdon, Oxon OX14 4RN

and by Routledge
605 Third Avenue, New York, NY 10158

Routledge is an imprint of the Taylor & Francis Group, an informa business

© 2024 Kate Lafferty

The right of Kate Lafferty to be identified as author of this work has been asserted in accordance with sections 77 and 78 of the Copyright, Designs and Patents Act 1988.

British Library Cataloguing-in-Publication Data
A catalogue record for this book is available from the British Library

Library of Congress Cataloging-in-Publication Data
Names: Lafferty, Kate, author.
Title: The teacher's guide to gifted and talented education : practical strategies for the classroom / Kate Lafferty.
Description: First edition. | New York : Routledge, 2024. | Includes bibliographical references and index. |Identifiers: LCCN 2023010205 (print) | LCCN 2023010206 (ebook) | ISBN 9781032213521 (hbk) | ISBN 9781032213514 (pbk) | ISBN 9781003267973 (ebk)
Subjects: LCSH: Gifted children--Education--United States. | Talented students--Education--United States. | Special education--United States.
Classification: LCC LC3993.9 .L335 2024 (print) | LCC LC3993.9 (ebook) | DDC 371.95--dc23/eng/20230505
LC record available at https://lccn.loc.gov/2023010205
LC ebook record available at https://lccn.loc.gov/2023010206

ISBN: 978-1-032-21352-1 (hbk)
ISBN: 978-1-032-21351-4 (pbk)
ISBN: 978-1-003-26797-3 (ebk)

DOI: 10.4324/9781003267973

Typeset in Galliard
by KnowledgeWorks Global Ltd.

For my colleagues and students,
Past, present, and future

Contents

List of tables and figures

List of tables

List of figures

Preface

Allow me to introduce myself...and this book

This book has been brewing in my head for several years now. It has been influenced and shaped by my experiences with colleagues, students, and families. I 'fell into' Gifted Education after being given the role of providing extension to students when I returned to teaching part-time from family leave. I had always been conscious of the learners in my classroom that were clearly highly able. As I began to read to find out the best ways of providing 'extension', I was hit with feelings of delight as well as a bit of embarrassment. Delight in that I used many of the recommended, evidence-based practices, like providing differentiated tasks that tapped into learner interests. And embarrassed at some of my less informed decisions like a complete lack of differentiation after lunch when integrated units were usually taught.

One of my frustrations was how difficult it seemed to be to find everything I wanted to know in one place or trying to understand how American-focused books related to an Australian setting. With a lot of research behind paywalls or in expensive, academic-focused books, access to current recommendations and information was challenging.

Once I had a handle on it, and knew I could help other teachers, and parents, I began offering workshops through our local government school network, mostly for free, or for a very cheap rate. This book is a way of continuing the conversations from those workshops.

I hope this book will serve you in the ways I was searching for when I began in this field. I hope you find it practical, relevant, and interesting with materials and templates that you can apply immediately as well as provoke bigger conversations within your school. My aim is to offer you with a way of thinking about developing the talents of students, at all year levels, in all learning domains, and in all contexts. Whether you are a teacher in a Gifted Ed withdrawal program, in a government, Catholic, or independent school, this book will be appropriate for you. Each chapter concludes with a reflection, an opportunity for you to reflect on any new understandings and your current practice. It can be used as an individual exercise or within your teaching teams. Developing my understandings in Gifted Education made me a better teacher for all students, not just those with high ability.

Throughout the book, you will find quotes and vignettes from high-ability students, their parents, and gifted adults. These are not designed to be representative of all high-ability students and families; however, they do offer genuine perspectives on their experiences at school and beyond. They capture a range of diverse views including neurodiversity, sexuality and gender diversity, indigenous, socioeconomic, and educational settings and types of provision offered. I am grateful for their generosity in sharing these personal, and at times painful, reflections. I have learnt so much from conversations with students and what works, or doesn't work. They are conversations well worth having.

The book is structured in a way that allows you to dip in and out with chapters based on challenges that come up time and again in classrooms. Each chapter is divided into two main sections (Back to Basics and Taking it Further) where depending on your level of interest, and time available, you can choose how in depth you want to go: a teachers' 'Choose your own Adventure' book for Gifted Education.

A note about terminology

Gifted, talented, high potential, high ability…

The use of these terms can be confusing and challenging. Challenging because there seem to be many ways of interpreting each of them and for 'gifted' in particular, there can be a negative reaction to it. When 'gifted' is used, it can create a sense of elitism for some, a sense of 'better than others'. This can be seen in comments like, 'all children are gifted in their own way', or some children's 'gifts' take longer to present than others.

The confusion comes from inconsistent use of the terms. In some cases, they are used interchangeably, treated as synonyms. In others, they have very clear, specific definitions, for example, you can't call a child gifted unless you

Table 0.1 Terminology used by Australian states and territories in Gifted Education

ACT	Gifted	Talented
New South Wales	Gifted, highly gifted	High potential
Northern Territory	Gifted	Talented
Queensland	Gifted	Talented
South Australia	Gifted	Talented
Tasmania	Gifted	Talented or highly able
Victoria	Highly able (includes high potential and/or performance)	
Western Australian	Gifted	Talented

have an assessment (e.g., WISC) that proves it. Table 0.1 shows the terminology used by different states and territories across Australia. All except Victoria use different terms to differentiate between giftedness and talent, with talent being synonymous with highly able or high potential.

Throughout this book, I have used high ability and high potential interchangeably. They are used to describe students who are typically described as 'gifted' or 'talented' in the Gifted Education literature.

I use Gifted Education to describe the provision and ways of working with this group of learners that provide them with the appropriate challenge and support and take into account typical characteristics of these learners.

Acknowledgements

This book is a result of working with colleagues, students, and families over many years and in many settings. It has been a privilege to work with so many high-ability students and their families. Some of their voices feature throughout this book adding their own personal insights and experiences and for that I am deeply grateful. To Synthia, Rowan, Steph, and Ella, thank you for your honest, constructive, and considered perspectives. I consider myself lucky to have been able to work with you and learn from you and I look forward to seeing how your futures unfold. Over the years, I have formed many wonderful relationships with families. Thank you for your openness and support over the years. To Teresa, Sally, Kenny, Monira, and Jodie, your perspectives as parents throughout this book bring this important parent-teacher relationship to life, reminding us that teachers are not just working with students, rather we work in partnership with families. To Dan, Michael, and Greg, as the voices of gifted adults, thank you for sharing your vulnerabilities and reflecting on your experiences (some not so pleasant) to better inform us of what happens beyond school. Your reflections on how your educational experiences impacted your life well-beyond Year 12 highlight the importance of Gifted Education. A huge thanks to my colleague and friend, Jo. As an experienced professional, your comments and feedback throughout the drafting process of this book were greatly appreciated. Thank you for your partnership, collaboration, inspiration, and support over the years.

Melissa Barnes, thanks for keeping me on track and for saying the right thing at the right time to get me over the finish line.

Without Vilija Stephens, I'm not sure I would have had the confidence to embark on this process. Thank you for your encouragement and taking a chance on this first-time author.

Georgia, thanks for patiently addressing all of my questions!

And to my family, Mick, Annie, and Emily, their support for all of my endeavours is unwavering, allowing me time to write, even on family holidays. Their engagement in discussions with me when I was unsure of the direction I should take at various times in the chapters allowed me to find clarity.

1

Theory Foundation of Practice

BACK TO BASICS

All good practices must be informed by an empirical and theoretical foundation. This ensures a rigorous and defensible approach in which schools can confidently and accurately identify and explain the why behind the how of their Gifted Education practices. This chapter provides an overview of a range of theoretical frameworks that are often seen as competing including: Gagné's Differentiated Model of Giftedness and Talent (DMGT); Actiotope Model of Giftedness; Sternberg's ACCEL (Active Concerned Citizenship and Ethical Leadership) Model; Renzulli's Three-Ring Conception of Giftedness; and the domain-specific Talent Development Megamodel (TDMM). The beginning of this chapter focuses on the two most common models in Australia, the DMGT and the three-ring conception of giftedness. Each framework is introduced and described separately with key aspects and implications identified and discussed.

TAKING IT FURTHER

This section provides a discussion of additional theories and models that are less well-known in Australian schools but with each having value: Actiotope Model of Giftedness; Sternberg's ACCEL (Active Concerned Citizenship and Ethical Leadership) Model; and the domain-specific TDMM. A summary of each theory is provided in table format for ease of comparison and implications for practice.

DOI: 10.4324/9781003267973-1

My experience with Gifted Education began when I returned to teaching from a short stint of family leave and was tasked by my principal to offer an extension programme for two days a week, in a primary school in Melbourne. This was not only an exciting but also rather daunting prospect, as I needed to make several decisions about what this extension programme might look like; who would I teach? What would I teach? When would I teach it? How do I teach it?

After a lot of reading, I proposed a model that addressed each of these questions. There were two notable reactions from the principal.

1. Who was going to field the questions from parents? He was concerned that the minute we started talking about 'extension' and withdrawing students from classes, there would be an avalanche of phone calls from parents demanding (a) their child be included in the extension programme, and (b) demanding to know why their child was NOT included.
2. A dismissal of the word 'gifted' as he thought that all parents think their child is gifted and that we are all gifted in our own way.

My response was to direct them to me, and I will answer all their phone calls and emails. I was confident that I could defend my decisions and communicate the reasons behind them. My confidence stemmed from one thing: I had based everything I was doing on theory and research. I used the terms 'gifted' and 'talented' when talking to colleagues, parents, and students. Based on theory, I sought a *shared understanding* of how we were going to use these terms to have a common language. Based on theory and research, I used a process for identifying students that would benefit from participating in an extension programme.

Teachers use theories and research to inform their practice every day. We draw on high-impact teaching strategies (HITS) because of their proven effectiveness. We use our knowledge of learning and developmental theories to ensure our teaching is appropriate and facilitates learning. We use Bloom's taxonomy to elicit higher levels of thinking. We encourage a growth mindset over one that is fixed. To work effectively with gifted and talented students, and their families, we need to understand the theories and research we can use to shape what and how we work with individual students each day. With this understanding, we are in a much better position to not only make defensible and justifiable decisions but to also make a big difference in the learning and school experiences of this cohort of students.

So many theories …

Gifted Education has no shortage of theories and theorists, with each offering valuable insights and guidance to teachers. Once you start looking for definitions and 'how to' guides, these insights can become overwhelming. What has always struck me is the ways in which these theories and frameworks are usually presented separately. For me, this implied that I needed to choose one, and hope that I chose the 'right' or 'best' one. With experience, I learned we can combine these theories and frameworks to suit our purpose and context – as long as it is informed and defensible.

The following section introduces two key and common theories and the discussion for each is based on the questions we need to be able to defend, as defined below. The *Taking it Further* section introduces three additional, and perhaps lesser known, models for giftedness and talent development. All five theories are summarized in a table at the end of this chapter.

- Who are we targeting?
- What are we going to teach?
- How are we going to teach it?
- When are we going to teach it?
- Why are we teaching this group in this way?

Differentiating Model of Giftedness and Talent

Gagné's Differentiating Model of Giftedness and Talent (DMGT) (Figure 1.1) is a framework that has many appealing features for teachers. It is often referred to as the most widely adopted and applied framework across Australia's education jurisdictions. However, there are questions about how well this model is understood and appropriately applied.[1]

Who are we targeting?

The DMGT was the model I drew on when first establishing a Gifted Education programme. The most appealing feature for me was that it provided a clear definition of, and distinction between, giftedness and talent. These words are often used interchangeably and there is still no agreement

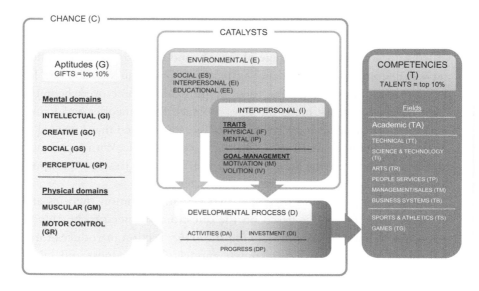

Figure 1.1 Gagné's Differentiating Model of Giftedness and Talent (DMGT)

Source: Gagné (2020)

in the field as to how these terms should be defined. Consider the following definition:

> Giftedness is greater awareness, a greater sensitivity, and a greater ability to understand and transform perceptions into intellectual and emotional experiences[2]

This is a wonderful way of capturing the essence of giftedness, but as teachers, how do we use this to inform our practice, to justify our decisions, our provision? Gagné's[3] definitions as per the DMGT have more utility:

> Giftedness (G) designates the possession and use of biologically anchored and informally developed outstanding natural abilities or aptitudes (called gifts), in at least one ability domain, to a degree that places an individual at least among the top 10% of age peers

> Talent designates the outstanding mastery of systematically developed competencies (knowledge and skills) in at least one field of human activity to a degree that places an individual at least among the top

10% of 'learning peers', namely, those having accumulated a similar amount of learning time from either current or past training.

(p. 80)

These definitions can be used as a shared language in our contexts. They distinguish between gifted and talented students and therefore can provide guidelines when determining whom we are targeting. But what do these definitions mean? For that, we need to look at the whole model of the DMGT.

The DMGT is a talent development model, and as such identifies the components of transforming natural abilities into competencies. Through each component, we can better understand the barriers and enablers that will affect the process of talent development and provide us with a roadmap that helps determine the 'what' and 'why' of provision.

The DMGT recognizes both mental and physical domains of natural abilities, ranging from intellectual to motor control. It is important to note that natural abilities are not equal to innate abilities. A key assumption of this model is that natural abilities need to be systematically developed. No one is born as a world-class athlete or mathematician. Rather, people may have an *aptitude* in one or more of the domains identified in the model, and it is only through a *learning process* that these aptitudes are realized as competencies or achievements.

By including a percentage in both definitions (i.e., the top 10%), we also have a range to help identify the students we wish to target. Prevalence measures differ across models and jurisdictions, but for the DMGT, the minimum threshold of the top 10% simplifies matters for schools in Australia and elsewhere that do not have wide-spread intelligence testing – a criterion that is used in the United States.[4] It would be naïve to think that all students in the top 10% are the same, exemplified by the news stories about the incredible academic achievements of young children, such as the 9-year-old who completed a bachelor's degree in electrical engineering in 9 months.[5] Whilst these stories are remarkable, they can do a disservice in shaping thinking about how we implicitly define gifted and talented students. Of course, these implicit beliefs then influence who, amongst our students, we believe needs additional provision. I have run workshops with experienced teachers who believed they have never taught a gifted or talented student in their class, because of the 'genius' image portrayed in the media. The DMGT offers a way of perceiving levels of giftedness through prevalence,[6] as shown in Table 1.1.

Table 1.1 DMGT system of levels within gifted or talented populations[6]

Label	Percentage (%)	Ratio
Mildly	10	1:10
Moderately	1	1:100
Highly	.1	1:1,000
Exceptionally	.01	1:10,000
Extremely	.001	1:100,000

By delineating levels, we can begin to describe the degrees of giftedness or talent of students and reorient thinking away from the media exceptionalities to a more common level that we will come across in our classrooms. With these levels, we have expanded the language that we can use with our colleagues, parents, and school communities to help define and describe our targeted student population.

What and how?

The scope of domains covered in the DMGTs natural abilities allows for an extensive range of aptitudes to be recognized and valued equally. The ability of a school to cater for all domains may neither be possible, nor desirable. However, the DMGT provides a way of communicating this to all stakeholders to say that these aptitudes are recognized, however, given resource constraints (personnel, time, money, expertise), we are focusing on the domains of a, b, and c.

This model is all about systematic talent development, and providing a structured developmental process to transform natural abilities into competencies that include both knowledge and skills.[4] The subcomponents of this are described in the Developmental Process (D) (see Figure 1.1) and consist of: Activities (DA); Investment (DI); and Progress (DP), each with a nested set of factors that need to be addressed for the process of developing talent to occur.[6] Starting with Activities, there needs to first be access to systematic learning. Students need to be identified or selected (see Chapter 2) to work on a set of structured activities. This may be through a child participating in a coding challenge and showing an aptitude in this area that is then nurtured or developed through more structured and deliberate coding classes. Or it may be ethical thinking that is nurtured and developed through intentional ethical decision-making/reasoning lessons. For teachers, the focus and ability to identify aptitudes will probably fall within or across academic domains. The instructor (e.g., coach, tutor, teacher) then sets about providing the content that needs to be learned, the developmental sequence in which it should be learned, and the format in which it should be taught, for talent development to occur. This forms the 'what'.

Of course, this deliberate process and provision of developmental activities does not magically just happen. It requires an investment of time, money, and energy. If there is one student in a Year 1 class who is a gifted or talented mathematician, then time and energy will need to be spent planning and delivering content for that one child to meet their developmental needs. Their progress (P), that is the stages of learning, the pace at which the student is learning, and recognizing turning points will be determining factors in shaping the 'what' and the level of investment required.

Another useful aspect of the DMGT, are the intrapersonal and environmental catalysts that recognize several factors that will enhance or detract from the talent development process. Beginning with environmental (E) catalysts, the model identifies milieu, individual and resources as subcomponents that influence an individual's talent development. The model recognizes that milieu (EM), i.e., where a student lives (metropolitan, regional, rural, or remote), socioeconomic status, cultural, social, and political climates are all influences in the degree to which a student has access to developmental activities. The individual (EI) environmental catalysts recognize the role that parents, family, peers, teachers, and mentors play in supporting talent development. The final environmental subcomponent is that of resources (ER) and includes access to an appropriate curricula and pedagogical approaches, groupings, or placement in teams.

Intrapersonal catalysts recognize the attributes and attitudes the individual brings to the talent development process. Divided into two dimensions (Traits and Goal Management) this set of catalysts includes aspects of physical and mental traits (such as health, disabilities, temperament, personality, and resilience) as well as awareness, motivation, and volition. Talent development is not a passive process, something that is done to the learner. Rather the learner is an active player that requires support and appropriate resourcing to develop their abilities. A student in a classroom who has never experienced challenges may not know how to persevere on a difficult task, may not have developed the resilience to persist, or know how to deal with failure. Our role as teachers, mentors, and perhaps family, is to support the learner in developing these attributes to facilitate the process.

This model supports learners and their talent development through

a. providing a distinction between gifted and talented, and a threshold that will assist teachers in recognizing students with the most need
b. identifying and acknowledging a range of natural abilities
c. recognizing the catalysts that will support and hinder this development and highlighting areas in which to provide support where possible
d. developing a systematic process of developmental activities and investing the resources required to do this.

Renzulli's Three-Ring Conception of Giftedness

Renzulli's model of giftedness recognizes that development of abilities occurs over time, and giftedness is not just an IQ score. This conception of giftedness was developed as part of the Schoolwide Enrichment Model (SEM). The SEM is a talent development approach that is used in schools globally. It is important to recognize that this approach is part of a larger model that encompasses identification and programming.

Who are we targeting?

This model recognizes two broad categories of giftedness: academic and creative-productive.[7] Academic giftedness is realized through high levels of academic achievement within a school context with learners doing well on achievement and cognitive tests. Creative-productive giftedness refers to those who are producers of knowledge, whether that be through creative contributions to art, culture, or knowledge.

The three-ring conception identifies three core clusters (rings) of traits that contribute to both academic and creative-productive giftedness, i.e., above-average ability, task commitment, and creativity. Above-average ability encompasses both the general abilities seen in aptitude tests (e.g., reasoning, memory, and abstract thinking) as well as more specific abilities associated with a specialized field (e.g., leadership, mathematics, and ballet). Not all the skills and knowledge associated with specific abilities are easily assessable. Above average in this context refers to the potential to have, or have demonstrated, high levels of performance, i.e., within the top 15–20%. Task commitment is about the motivation and attention directed towards a specific task. Task commitment can be seen in the idea of grit (perseverance and passion),[8] dedicated practice and self-efficacy. Creativity includes traits of curiosity, novelty, flow,[9] originality, and ingenuity. It also includes a willingness to challenge the status quo of traditional ideas and processes.

The definition of giftedness comes from an amalgamation of the three components (task commitment, above-average ability, creativity) with a focus on gifted *behaviours* that demonstrate all three clusters of traits, with the *interaction* of these traits being of most interest. With this in mind, we can assume that we may see gifted behaviours in classrooms some of the time, but not all the time. The demonstration of behaviours will be dependent on many factors unique to the person, circumstance, context and conditions. A gifted or talented child can be described as one who displays these traits, or has the potential to develop and apply them to a valued domain.

What and how?

If adopting this model, it is important to provide a wide range of opportunities that allow students to demonstrate gifted behaviours. For this reason, Renzulli suggests working with the top 20% of students who have been identified through a range of different measures. This may be interpreted to mean a greater level of prevalence for identifying and working with students, however, when considered with the SEM, and the definition described above, we can see the importance of casting such a wide net in providing opportunities for a larger number of students. As with all learning in a classroom, if we do not offer students a variety of opportunities (mode and number) to demonstrate learning and potentiality, we are limiting their chance to demonstrate their gifted behaviours. An example of this was when I worked with a group of students in Years 3–6 (9–12 years old) to design and construct a solar-powered boat. In small teams, they chose the materials and used a range of tools in the construction process, including a soldering iron. One student demonstrated a great aptitude and interest in wiring and then requested a soldering iron for a Christmas gift! It sparked an interest in her and allowed her to demonstrate gifted behaviours that may have remained untapped. In many cases, schools are probably already offering clubs of some sort where potentiality can be discovered.

Both the DMGT and SEM are supported by research and have been used widely around the world. This introduction provides an overview of both models, and there are freely available resources, readings and slides and presentations available on the following websites:

- Differentiating model of gifts and talents: https://gagnefrancoys.wixsite.com/dmgt-mddt
- Renzulli Center for Creativity, Gifted Education, and Talent development: https://gifted.uconn.edu/

Taking it further

This section provides an introduction to an additional three theories that are not as well known or widely applied in Australian contexts, but each offer interesting insights and considerations for Gifted Education in schools.

Active Concerned Citizenship and Ethical Leadership (ACCEL) and transformational giftedness

Sternberg's ACCEL Model views giftedness and the purpose of Gifted Education as developing active concerned citizens and ethical leaders.[10] There is a distinction between transformational giftedness and transactional giftedness with transformational focused on making the world a better place, in some way, and the latter an exchange-based approach where the gifted learner is expected to both give and receive (e.g., receive a scholarship and then perform highly in academic measures).[11]

Who (and what) are we targeting?

Rather than focusing on cognitive assessments and standardized tests to identify giftedness or high levels of ability, this model proposes that we look for four competencies that are characteristic of expert real-world problem solvers:

1. Critical thinking (analytical thinking)
2. Creativity
3. Common sense (practical intelligence)
4. Wisdom and ethics

Sternberg's argument is based on the wicked problems that confront our world. Problems, such as climate change, prevention of epidemics and pandemics, dependency on finite energy resources, income disparity and wealth distribution are complex and difficult, and not new. However, regardless of the intelligence of the people working on them, they have yet to be solved. Simply put, intelligence is not enough.

The competencies listed above will be familiar to many teachers as they are included in varying degrees in education jurisdictions around the world.[12] The exception is common sense, or practical intelligence, which is 'what one needs to know to succeed in life that typically is not explicitly taught and that even is not often verbalized' (p. 161).[13] Practical intelligence does not come hand in hand with IQ, but if common sense is displayed in one area, it will likely also be evident in another area.

The assumption underpinning this model is that these competencies are teachable and assessable. The ACCEL model provides a way of developing leadership amongst high-ability students – the cohort we often label as being the 'future leaders'. This model views intelligence as developing expertise in a domain that requires metacognitive skills; learning skills; thinking skills; knowledge; and motivation and highlights the limitations of the types of abilities that are identified and valued through traditional Western testing that favours analytical skills.[14] Given this perspective, Sternberg doesn't discern different levels of abilities, rather all ability levels are seen as various stages of developing expertise. The distinction made between gifted and non-gifted individuals is reflected in the rate and/or level of learning, which is both faster and higher.[15]

Talent Development Megamodel

The Talent Development Megamodel (TDMM)[16] can be seen as an integrated approach that draws on a range of theories and models. This model defines giftedness as '...the manifestation of performance that is clearly at the upper end of the distribution in a talent domain...' (p. 103).[17] Again, as with all talent development models, there is an assumption of the development of expertise in a domain. The potential is recognized as the starting point for giftedness that transforms into achievement and then once talents are fully developed, eminence becomes the measuring stick.

As with other models, the TDMM consists of six elements[18] which can be considered observations or assumptions that underpin the model. These are summarized in Table 1.2.

There are clear practical implications of this model that affect identification and programming applications. Students need opportunities to demonstrate their potential, and programming needs to go beyond the

Table 1.2 Elements and descriptions of the Talent Development Megamodel

Elements of the TDMM	Description
1. Domain-specific abilities	General abilities and specialized, domain-specific abilities are required in order to develop talent, with general abilities playing a more important role in the early years and domain-specific abilities becoming increasing necessary for developing expertise.
2. Domain-specific developmental trajectories	The developmental trajectory for domains varies with different starting points (age) and peaks, with many academic trajectories starting in secondary school, whilst other domains (e.g., gymnastics) will begin much earlier and have an earlier peak.
3. Ability is malleable	The malleability of ability is an important assumption as it means that an observed absence of domain-specific skills doesn't mean that they will not develop, just that they haven't yet due to perhaps a lack of opportunity.
4. Psychosocial characteristics are essential and teachable	As expertise develops, so too does the need for psychosocial skills, such as growth mindset, resilience, goal setting, time management and organizational skills, self-efficacy/self-confidence, commitment, and coping with challenges.[19]
5. Opportunity must be available and taken	It stands to reason that for learners to develop expertise in a domain they need opportunities relevant to their stage of development. Some opportunities may be available through everyday schooling, others may require private access (e.g., sports, performing arts). As an opportunity is offered, it also needs to be accepted by a learner.
6. Creative productivity in adulthood and eminence are the desired outcomes	Eminence is the long-term outcome of Gifted Education in this model. Even though teachers in primary and secondary schools will not be actively providing input in the later stages of the developmental trajectory, they still need to be aware of what that trajectory looks like to support their students appropriately.

knowledge, skills and understandings of the domain, and also includes explicit teaching of psychosocial skills.

Actiotope Model of Giftedness

The Actiotope Model of Giftedness (AMG) approaches talent development by focusing on the relationship between the learner and the learner's environment.[20] The term 'actiotope' refers to the environment (material, social, informational) of the individual, as well as the individual.[21] The utility of this theoretical approach is that it can ultimately be seen as a theory of achievement, and therefore appropriate for all students.[22] Giftedness is not about gifts and talents, but rather whether students can learn in an effective way to develop expertise leading to eminence through an identified learning pathway.[23]

The actiotope model places 'action' at the centre of talent development. However, the model encourages the examination of not just the individual, but rather the interactions between environments and the individual in determining 'actions', and the possibilities for action. This is not necessarily a new concept in achievement-related models, as we have seen a similar approach in the DMGT, but this model provides us with a way of both identifying and describing the catalysts in more detail.

The dynamic actiotope consists of four interactive components: the action repertoire; the environment; the subjective space; and goals.[24] The action repertoire is made up of the actions currently available to the student, such as the ability to recognize common fractions (halves, quarters) for a student in Year 2 and being able to solve a problem involving ratios for a Year 8 student. In other words, you can't use or apply skills and knowledge that you do not yet have. The student will draw on the action that matches both their goal and the perceived previous success they have had with that action. The environment is important as it permits or facilitates the action of the learner. The environment can be either external or internal (i.e., within the individual) and each consists of resources, called capital, that will support the learner in their talent development. This separation of internal and external factors is reminiscent of the DMGT's catalysts. Broadly, external resources are described as *educational capital* and an individual's internal resources are termed *learning capital*, with each type of capital consisting of subcomponents. It is the separation and identification of resources that I think holds the most value for schools in applying the AMG. Table 1.3 describes the sub-types of both educational and learning capitals.

Table 1.3 Actiotope model learning and educational resources

Educational capital	Description	Learning capital	Description
Economic	The financial resources available to spend on commencing and continuing learning and educational processes, e.g., school fees, tutors, or government expenditure on education	Organismic	The health and well-being of the learner that determines the degree to which they can engage in the learning process, e.g., an illness that leads to prolonged absence from school
Infrastructural	The organizational and structural resources that facilitate learning and education such as school libraries, a quiet study space at home	Actional	The action repertoire of a learner includes the knowledge, skills, and physical characteristics that determine the range of available actions
Cultural	Refers to the culture of the family, school, community, and society, and the models, systems of thinking that will facilitate or hamper learning	Telic	Refers to goal setting and includes functional learning goals as well as planned conditions for meeting a learner's needs
Social	Refers to the direct or indirect influence of peers, family members, teachers, and mentors in the success of learning and educational processes	Attentional	Refers to the learner's ability to remain focused, qualitatively and quantitatively, to be productive
Didactic	The quality of teaching and curriculum – the 'know-how' of those responsible for planning and implementing learning and educational instruction	Episodic	A learner's ability to know what skills and knowledge to draw on in a given context that is appropriate for both situation and goal

In a school context, understanding that these resources play an important part in a learner's level of achievement in school is both informative and practical. Teachers can identify the degrees of both educational and learning capital resources and where there may be deficits, take action to address or compensate for these. We see some of these issues already being addressed for students such as homework clubs to provide support and a quiet place to study.

The framework can be used to work with colleagues and families and used as a basis to develop (and audit) support plans. Consider the high-ability student who manages to navigate their way successfully through school until they reach the upper secondary years. Using this framework, teachers can look at the system within which the learner is operating and identify the capitals that need additional development. Perhaps this is due to low levels of attentional capital – the student has never learned the strategies to remain focused as previous learning experiences haven't required it. Perhaps there were some mental health issues that are impacting their organismic capital. We cannot separate the learner from the environment and this model helps remind us that the person-environment interactions need to be considered when working with any group of learners.

Summary

This chapter has introduced five different theories and approaches to giftedness and talent development. The common themes across these models include:

1. The development of abilities and talents requires a deliberate, systematic approach
2. The learner needs support in developing not only their talents, but also their intrapersonal skills (e.g., motivation, resilience, goal setting)
3. Talent development requires resources (the AMG breaks these resources down into practical categories)
4. Talent development is a long-term process.

Differences in the models occur in

1. Definitions
2. Ways of identifying and prevalence (e.g., consider the ACCEL model and the TDMM)
3. The end goal of talent development (e.g., development of excellence in the AMG, and the ability to make a positive impact in the ACCEL transformational model).

There is no one 'right' model or approach that should be used. Each model has its supporters and detractors. This is where it can become confusing and tempting to put it in the too hard basket. The challenge is working out which model resonates with you and your context. Table 1.4 provides a summary of the theories and the ways in which they will guide your practice. Whatever is decided can then be shared with the school community and form the basis of policy development, implementation, etc.

Practical tips

1. If you are working on your own, or leading this in your school, try and find another school that has an established practice that you can visit or speak with for ideas and advice
2. There are a lot of freely available readings on the internet. Use Google Scholar to access research articles or more detailed descriptions of the theory. Some are behind a paywall; others have accessible PDFs.
3. Check your Department of Education's online resources, as well as other states/territories regarding the models they use.
4. Share the model/s with your team and discuss which one is most appropriate for your school community, or how you might use elements of each.

Table 1.4 Summary of theories and implications

Theory	Definition of giftedness	Identification	Programming	Example
DMGT	Distinction between giftedness and talent Definitions provided for both	Top 10% for potential (age peers) identifiable through aptitude measures Top 10% for achievement (amount of experience) identifiable through achievement	Providing learners with appropriate activities (content, pace, format), time and support to systematically develop domain-specific abilities	Differentiating the learning for the student in the regular classroom using evidence of what they already know and what they need to learn next, rather than a one size fits all or many models
AMG	A label that is applied to individuals for whom we can identify a pathway to eminence Focus is on the action, not intelligence measures	No prevalence estimates Identification can be based on learning orientation (a questionnaire)[25]	A planned, holistic approach for the systematic development of action repertoire with a focus on supporting the development of excellence	Developing an individual learning plan (longer term) outlining a clear pathway of what will be done, how the learner will be supported and how the resources required will be supplied and maintained
Three-ring conception of giftedness	Someone who displays or has the potential to display the composite set of traits of above-average ability, task commitment, and creativity. Distinguishes between school-house giftedness and creative-productive giftedness	Top 20% of students who have been identified through a range of measures (achievement tests, teacher/self/parent nomination, assessment of potential creativity, and ability to commit to a task) These students form the 'talent pool'	Forms the basis of the Schoolwide Enrichment Model (SEM), used as a whole-school model that includes regular classroom activities, enrichment clusters, and special services Students can complete a 'profiler' and develop a Total Talent Portfolio of work samples	Three tiers of activities are offered both within the regular classroom and in small groups: Type I: General exploratory activities (e.g., guest speakers, excursions) to expose students to new areas/disciplines beyond the curriculum Type II: Group training activities (e.g., problem-solving, creative, and critical thinking) Type III: Individual and small group investigations of real problems (most advanced level of enrichment)

(Continued)

Table 1.4 (Continued)

Theory	Definition of giftedness	Identification	Programming	Example
TDMM	High levels of performance in a talent domain that is demonstrated by only a few	No prevalence estimates, but as students need to be at the upper end of the distribution, this could be implied as being the top 5%	Domain-specific opportunities to practice and develop in a specific area, will also include explicit teaching of time management, resilience, coping with challenges, etc.	Withdrawal Maths programme working with a mentor to extend knowledge and skills, and entry into Australian Maths Trust competitions used for talent identification and invitations to higher level competitions and camps
ACCEL	Giftedness as developing expertise; from novice to exemplary achievement (possibly an infinite developmental trajectory). Distinguishes between transactional and transformational giftedness with the latter focused on making a positive impact	No prevalence estimates (e.g., top X%) Use a battery of measures to assess creativity, critical thinking, common sense, ethical thinking, and wisdom	Opportunities provided for explicit teaching and development of analytical, creative, practical and wise thinking	Design thinking project focusing on one of the Sustainable Development Goals Future Problem Solving Program

Chapter Reflection

1. How do you define or describe
   - Gifted
   - Talented
   - High ability
   - High potential
2. Does your school have a shared understanding of the terms?
3. Which of the models presented in this chapter resonate with you and why?
4. How would you describe this model to your colleagues/students/families?

Notes

1 Merrotsy, P. (2017). Gagné's Differentiated Model of Giftedness and Talent in Australian education. *Australasian Journal of Gifted Education*, 26, 29–42. https://doi.org/10.21505/ajge.2017.0014

2 Roeper, A. (1982). How the gifted cope with their emotions. *Roeper Review*, 5(2), 21–24. https://doi.org/10.1080/02783198209552672

3 Gagné, F. (2021). Implementing the DMGT's constructs of giftedness and talent: What, why, and how? *Handbook of giftedness and talent development in the Asia-Pacific* (pp. 71–99).

4 Gagné, F. (1998). A proposal for subcategories within gifted or talented populations. *Gifted Child Quarterly*, 42(2), 87–95. https://doi.org/10.1177/001698629804200203

5 Deutsch, A. (2019, November 22). Belgian boy on track to become world's youngest university graduate. *Reuters*. https://www.reuters.com/article/us-netherlands-prodigy-idUSKBN1XV1JO

6 Gagné, F. (2018). Academic talent development: Theory and best practices. In *APA handbook of giftedness and talent* (pp. 163–183). https://doi.org/10.1037/0000038-011

7 Renzulli, J. S., & Reis, S. M. (2018). The three-ring conception of giftedness: A developmental approach for promoting creative productivity in young people. In *APA handbook of giftedness and talent* (pp. 185–199). American Psychological Association. https://doi.org/10.1037/0000038-012

8 Duckworth, A. (2016). *Grit: The power of passion and perseverance* (Vol. 234). Scribner.

9 Csikszentmihalyi, M. (1990). *Flow: The psychology of optimal experience*. Harper & Row.

10 Sternberg, R. J. (2017). ACCEL: A New Model for Identifying the Gifted. *Roeper Review, 39*(3), 152–169. https://doi.org/10.1080/02783193.2017.1318658

11 Sternberg, R. J. (2020). Transformational giftedness: Rethinking our paradigm for gifted education. *Roeper Review, 42*(4), 230–240.

12 Taylor, R., Fadel, C., Kim, H., & Care, E. (2020). *Competencies for the 21st Century*. Center for Curriculum Redesign, and Brookings Institution.

13 Sternberg, R. J. (2017). ACCEL: A new model for identifying the gifted. *Roeper Review, 39*(3), 152–169. https://doi.org/10.1080/02783193.2017.1318658

14 Sternberg, R. J. (1999). Intelligence as developing expertise. *Contemporary Educational Psychology, 24*(4), 359–375. https://doi.org/10.1006/ceps.1998.0998

15 Sternberg, R. J. (2001). Giftedness as developing expertise: A theory of the interface between high abilities and achieved excellence. *High Ability Studies, 12*(2), 159–179.

16 Subotnik, R. F., Olszewski-Kubilius, P., & Worrell, F. C. (2021). The Talent Development Megamodel: A domain-specific conceptual framework based on the psychology of high performance. In R. J. Sternberg & D. Ambrose (Eds.), *Conceptions of giftedness and talent* (pp. 425–442). Springer International Publishing. https://doi.org/10.1007/978-3-030-56869-6_24

17 Olszewski-Kubilius, P., Subotnik, R. F., Worrell, F. C., Wardman, J., Tan, L. S., & Lee, S.-Y. (2021). Sociocultural perspectives on the talent development megamodel. *Handbook of Giftedness and talent development in the Asia-Pacific* (pp. 101–127).

18 Ibid.

19 Olszewski-Kubilius, P., Subotnik, R. F., Davis, L. C., & Worrell, F. C. (2019). Benchmarking psychosocial skills important for talent development. *New Directions for Child and Adolescent Development, 2019*(168), 161–176.

20 Ziegler, A., & Baker, J. (2013). Talent development as adaptation: The role of educational and learning capital. In S. N. Phillipson, H. Stoeger, & A. Ziegler (Eds.), *Exceptionality in East Asia: Explorations in the Actiotope Model of Giftedness* (pp. 18–39). Routledge.

21 Ziegler, A., Vialle, W., & Wimmer, B. (2013). The Actiotope Model of Giftedness: An introduction to some central theoretical assumptions. In S. N. Phillipson, H. Stoeger, & A. Ziegler (Eds.), *Exceptionality in East Asia: Explorations of the Actiotope Model of Giftedness* (pp. 1–17). Routledge.

22 Lafferty, K., Phillipson, S. N., & Costello, S. (2020). Educational resources and gender norms: An examination of the Actiotope Model of Giftedness and social gender norms on achievement. *High Ability Studies* (pp. 1–17).

23 Ziegler, A., Stoeger, H., & Vialle, W. (2012). Giftedness and gifted education: The need for a paradigm change. *Gifted Child Quarterly, 56*(4), 194–197.

24 Ziegler, A., & Phillipson, S. N. (2012). Towards a systematic theory of giftedness. *High Ability Studies, 23*, 3–30.

25 Ziegler, A., & Stoeger, H. (2008). A learning oriented subjective action space as an indicator of giftedness. *Psychology Science, 50*(2), 222.

2 Identification or Selection?

BACK TO BASICS

Identifying learning needs is an essential first step in Gifted Education. However, many 'identification' practices are often methods of selection and are based on achievement data alone. This chapter highlights the need for identification practices to be informed by the underpinning theoretical framework. Connections to the frameworks discussed in Chapter 1 highlight the implications of each framework on identification practices. The difference between selection and identification will be discussed and a range strategies and examples to ensure a comprehensive approach to identification are introduced. This includes the use of parent checklists and student self-nomination forms.

TAKING IT FURTHER

This section provides additional discussion on the ways bias may impact identification practices when working with diverse learners and highlights real-life scenarios where bias can be present.

The ways in which a school responds to the who, what, when, and how of Gifted Education provision will largely determine whether selection or identification processes are used. It is important to recognize the difference between the two and the ramifications this has for the students who have a need for a gifted learning intervention and those who do not.

It's not uncommon for schools to use achievement data for selecting students for gifted or extension/enrichment classes and opportunities (e.g., one-off

DOI: 10.4324/9781003267973-2

events, competitions). This approach is quick and easy and provides a measure of objectivity. Norm-referenced tests are often used in schools for entire cohorts, and teachers can then use the rankings to select any number of students that meet their criteria for selection. However, when using achievement tests (commercial or in-house), selection is based on performance. High levels of performance on a well-constructed assessment can indicate high levels of knowledge, understanding, and application. However, an absence of high levels of performance does not necessarily mean an absence of high ability. This is true for all students, and particularly for students who are considered twice exceptional where they may have a physical disability or learning difficulty that prevents them from demonstrating their ability through traditional forms of assessment.

Conversely, *identification* implies a more considered effort in determining the learning needs of students. Rather than relying on achievement data, educators learn about their students' abilities and interests from a range of sources. This is a developmental approach that focuses on ensuring students are met at their point of need. Identifying learner needs means that the learning environment, content, process, and product can be organized to facilitate growth so that students can thrive. When identification occurs early (e.g., kindergarten), then interventions can begin early too.

Table 2.1 lists a range of identification and selection strategies that schools draw on when deciding on the 'who' of Gifted Education.

The range of instruments and strategies each have their advantages and disadvantages. For objectivity, commercially available tests provide reliable and valid results that can be trusted. But they come at a cost. There are some effective ways of managing this cost, such as using the commercial test as a last confirmatory step. There are also administrative considerations such as time, supervision, and training. For intelligence tests, they are administered by a psychologist in a one-on-one setting and are usually organized by families. The associated costs can be prohibitive for some families. Scholarship or high-ability testing is lengthy (2–3 hours) and there is a cost per student. Some schools and jurisdictions will offer these on a set date for large-scale testing and families need to register and pay in advance. These tests can also be used as a secondary measure to further distinguish between an already identified group.

A cheaper option that can be more practical in a school setting is using aptitude tests. Aptitude tests objectively assess reasoning skills. For educational purposes, verbal, numerical, spatial, and abstract reasoning can

Table 2.1 Identification and selection strategies

Strategy	Description	Example	Objective or subjective
Aptitude tests	Designed to measure potential for learning knowledge or acquiring skill	ACER General Ability Test (AGAT)	Objective
Achievement tests	Measure the amount of learning gained, standardized, reliable, and valid	Progressive Achievement Tests (PAT) in Reading/ Maths, NAPLAN	Objective
Academic grades	School-based, subject-specific, as captured in semester or continuous reporting	Students at least 12 months ahead of grade level	Will have varying degrees of subjectivity according to the nature of the assessments upon which the academic grade is based
Behavioural checklists – teacher	A checklist of indicative gifted and talented behaviours that teachers might observe in the classroom	Teacher behavioural checklist	Subjective
Competition results	International, national, or state competition results that provide the percentile rank for students	Australasian Problem Solving Mathematical Olympiads (APSMO) International Competitions and Assessments for Schools (ICAS)	Objective
Teacher nomination	Teachers complete a nomination form based on their observations of the student. Will often include a behavioural checklist or inventory to provide perspectives	May include the behavioural checklist as well as additional comments, observations	Subjective

(*Continued*)

Table 2.1 (Continued)

Strategy	Description	Example	Objective or subjective
Student self-nomination	Students may respond to a set of open-ended questions indicative of gifted and talented learners	Questionnaire, autobiography (with prompts), rating scales, application form to participate in a program	Subjective
Scholarship testing	Standardized norm-referenced tests	Edutest or school-administered ACER scholarship tests	Objective
Peer nomination	An informal strategy where students may be asked about who they approach to get help in various domains	Guess Who: Peer nomination Form[1] (I am thinking of someone who… Who am I thinking of?)	Subjective
Parent nomination	Parents respond to a set of open-ended questions indicative of gifted and talented learners	Sayler parent checklist	Subjective
Performance assessments/portfolios	Performances and products can be collated over time to reflect what the learner can do. Portfolios can be scholastic (e.g., writing, mathematics) or creative (e.g., music, drama, visual arts)	May be domain specific or span many learning areas.	Objective
Creative thinking tests	Tests designed to tap into creative thinking. May be verbal, figural, quantitative	Open-ended assessments captioning cartoons or generating novel solutions to scenario-based problems	Subjective
Rating scales	Norm-referenced scales that cover a range of domains	Gifted Rating Scales[2]	Subjective

(Continued)

Table 2.1 (Continued)

Strategy	Description	Example	Objective or subjective
High-ability selection tests	Commercially available standardized norm-referenced covering mathematical and abstract reasoning, reading comprehension, and written expression	ACER High Ability Selection Test – primary and secondary versions available[3]	Objective
Non-verbal intelligence tests	A standardized intelligence test that measures abstract reasoning as an estimate of fluid intelligence	Raven's 2[4]	Objective
Intelligence/ cognitive tests	Standardized tests that measure ability across a range of cognitive domains	Weschler Intelligence Scale-Children (WISC-5)[5] Stanford-Binet Intelligence Scales (SB-5)[6]	Objective
Off-level tests	Provide students with tests that are beyond their current grade level. This may be one, two, or many years above		Objective

inform teachers about a student's capacity to develop skills and knowledge. Whilst there are several aptitude tests freely available online, it may be difficult to ascertain how much you can trust the results. Therefore, to be certain of the measurement properties and subsequent interpretation and use of the results, it is preferred to use instruments that are well-designed, tested, and can be trusted. This usually comes at a cost, but a cost that can generally be absorbed by a school. An example of one that I used in a government primary school was the ACER General Ability Test (AGAT). This is a 50-minute online multiple-choice test that is easy to administer with current rates at less than $10 per student or cheaper for a 12-month licence.

Another objective tool for identification is achievement tests. As with any testing, there is a fundamental assumption that the test is both valid and reliable. Again, this often comes back to commercial products that schools already use routinely as part of their assessment and reporting practices. Tests such as ACER's Progressive Achievement Test (PAT) suite provide domain-specific information about a learner's current level of knowledge, understanding, and skills.

Subjective measures also range in administration costs and time. Tools such as The Gifted Rating Scales[7] have been used with several cultural groups[8]. For use with students aged six to 13 years and 11 months, there are six scales that cover the domains of intellectual, academic, motivation, creativity, leadership, and artistic talent. Younger children (four–six years and 11 months) are assessed on intellectual, academic readiness, motivation, creativity, and artistic talent. Teachers can complete these scales independently and online, but it does require knowledge of the learner's skills and behaviours to answer accurately. If using this type of tool, the time of year and the teacher's experience with the child need to be considered.

Additional subjective approaches to identifying gifted and talented students include behavioural checklists and parent/student nomination. There are some useful behavioural checklists that can be used, such as the teacher form that lists both positive and negative behaviours associated with a range of characteristics associated with gifted and talented children (see Box 2.1)[9]. In my experience, this has been a very useful checklist to use with teachers because it prompts teachers to consider learners who may be disruptive in class. There have been many times where teachers are introduced to this checklist and immediately start thinking about the learner who is easily distracted, or rushes through work. The framing of these behaviours in this way highlights the reasons why these behaviours may be occurring and may encourage the teacher to take another look at what might be going on for that student. As with the rating scale example, teacher checklists need to be completed by those who know the learner and have seen these behaviours manifest in different contexts and situations. This is not something a teacher could do at the beginning of the school year if they were just getting to know their class.

Teachers need to be trained in using these checklists before they begin filling them in. Training doesn't need to be onerous and can be conducted during a staff meeting or after-school professional learning session. Establishing the purpose of completing the checklist (how it will be used, by whom, how often they need to be completed) will ensure everyone is on the same page.

Box 2.1 Teacher nomination form

Student Name: _____ Year: _____

Teacher Name: _____ Date: _____

Highlight the subjects that you wish to nominate this student for:

Mathematics	Reading	Science	Writing/Research

Circle each behaviour you observe in the classroom or playground.

Characteristic	Positive Behaviours	Negative Behaviours
1. Highly curious	• asks lots of questions • is inquisitive • remembers details	• asks seemingly irrelevant questions • poor group participant • easily distracted from task
2. Abstract thinker	• makes generalizations • tests out ideas	• questions others • questions authority
3. Flexible thinker	• uses variety of strategies to work something out	• manipulates people and situations by using a variety of strategies
4. Clever use of humour	• enjoys 'adult' humour • gets teachers' jokes	• uses humour at the expense of others
5. Superior vocabulary	• high levels of engagement in discussions • enjoys adult-like discussions	• may be bossy or overbearing when working with others
6. Advanced reading	• reads widely • advanced vocabulary and comprehension	• reads constantly • neglects peer interaction and work – prefers to read
7. Retention of knowledge; fast learner	• learns content and skills quickly and easily • detailed recall of facts	• rushes work, then disrupts others • monopolizes class discussions
8. Long attention span	• maintains extended periods of concentration and focus on areas of interest	• easily distracted unless the task is an area of passion or interest

Characteristic	Positive Behaviours	Negative Behaviours
9. Independent	• self-directed • focused on task in research or study	• reduced involvement in discussion or group work • uncooperative in a group
10. High level of responsibility and commitment	• sets attainable goals • learns to accept own limitations • works with peers in a group	• self-critical • perfectionist when completing tasks • sets unrealistic expectations for self and/or other group members

Adapted from Merrick, C (2004) Adapted from Gross, MacLeod, Drummond & Merrick (2001), Clark (1983) and Baska (1989) in Merrick, C., & Targett, R. (2004) Gifted and talented education professional development package for teachers: Module 2 Primary. (Caroline Merrick, 2004)

A common question and/or misconception is that once the initial batch of checklists is completed (either for the first time or at a point in time each year), that the opportunity to nominate a child for that year has passed. This is a process that can and should be done at any time. One of the wonderful characteristics of a classroom is that you never know what will happen each day. You never know what students will demonstrate and if a teacher observes a behaviour they think might indicate high potential, this should be pursued. Box 2.2 provides instructions and training tips for teachers.

Box 2.2 Training tips and instructions for using a behavioural checklist

1. Determine how and where the information in the completed checklists will be used and stored. Will they be paper or digital versions? Who ensure the information is secure? What happens with the information in subsequent years?
2. Consider each characteristic independently of the others, and avoid ratings based on general impression of the student (i.e., halo effect).

3. Be conscious of norming. We often base judgements on the frequency or degree of the behaviour compared to other students in the class. However, as the composition of the class changes each year, so too will the comparison. As much as possible, base your judgement on what you have observed for that child.

4. Avoid the shopping list approach where a student is observed over a short period of time. Take a longer-term view and consider behaviours over an extended period.

5. Multiple raters are beneficial as it provides greater reliability.

6. These checklists should not be used on their own as the sole tool for identification or selection. Rather, they should be part of a battery of instruments.

Notes for Rating Scales

1. If using a rating scale, with 'always', 'rarely', etc., then base judgements on what is typically observed. There should be agreement amongst raters about what these descriptors mean prior to administering (i.e., moderate).

2. It is unlikely that students will be 'high' in all characteristics. If ratings are all high, or all low, this may be an indication the scale has not been completed with sufficient consideration.

Domain-specific behavioural checklists

The discussion so far has been very general in its nature, looking at typical behaviours (positive and negative) and common tools and strategies. Using general tools, such as the teacher version of the behaviour checklist, works well in primary school settings and has also been used effectively with secondary school teachers. However, for schools that are structured according to subjects, as many secondary schools are, having domain-specific behavioural checklists can be useful. The value of these lies in providing domain-specific behaviours that can be readily observed in the learning context and are based on teachers' experience with high-ability students[10].

The Purdue scales (see Table 2.2) are a rating scale and were designed to be completed using a four-point scale where each behaviour was assigned 1 (rarely, seldom or never), 2 (occasionally or sometimes), 3 (often or

Table 2.2 Purdue Academic Rating Scales[11] (adapted)

Mathematics	Science	English	Humanities
Generalizes mathematical relationships, relates concepts in various applications.	Good at verbalising science concepts, makes good oral presentations.	Interested in words, definitions, derivations; has an extensive vocabulary.	Reads widely on social issues from a variety of books, online media, or newspapers.
Organises data to discover patterns or relationships.	Interested in science books and television programs, enjoys science fiction.	Sees details, is a good observer, sees relationships, makes connections.	Becomes absorbed in the investigation of topics.
Persistent in learning math, concentrates, works hard, motivated, interested.	Has science hobbies, is a collector, likes gadgets.	Organises ideas and sequences well in preparation for speaking or writing.	Displays intellectual curiosity, becomes interested in a variety of topics not required or assigned.
Analyses problems carefully, considers alternatives, does not necessarily accept first answer.	Good at planning, designing, decision-making.	Has a good sense of humour; uses and understands satire, puns, and second meanings.	Skilled in analysing topics, finding the underlying problem, questioning, investigating.
Resourceful in seeking ways to solve a problem.	Sees connections, sees relationship of science to real world.	Reads widely for a period of time in a variety of types of literature; may focus on one type, then switch and focus on another.	Attracted towards cognitive complexity; enjoys puzzles, paradoxes, mysteries.
Interested in numbers and quantitative relationships, sees usefulness or applications of mathematics.	Organizes experiments, capable of separating and controlling variables.	Original and creative; comes up with unique ideas in writing or speaking.	Asks questions that are open-ended or philosophical.

(Continued)

Table 2.2 (Continued)

Mathematics	Science	English	Humanities
Learns math concepts and processes faster than other students.	Comes up with good questions or ideas for experiments.	Develops convincing characters and situations in writing.	Has a wide vocabulary which is used precisely and appropriately.
Good at verbalizing math concepts, processes, and solutions.	Good at exploring, questioning, investigating, studying things in detail.	Withholds judgement while investigating a topic; willing to explore a topic in greater depth than other students, curious.	Enjoys language, reading, conversation, listening, and verbal communication.
Identifies and restates problems, good at formulating hypotheses.	Good at visualizing, able to see complex patterns in ideas or dates.	Recognizes author's or speaker's point of view, mood, or intentions.	Sensitive to social issues, sees ethical and moral questions.
Reasons effectively.	Interested in numerical analysis, good at measurement and data analysis.	Elaborates well when speaking or writing, uses vivid expressions which make words 'come alive'.	Suspends judgement, entertains alternative explanations or points of view while exploring a question.
Enjoys trying to solve difficult problems, likes puzzles and logic problems.	Understands scientific method, able to formulate hypotheses and conduct experiments carefully.	Visualizes and translates images into written or spoken forms.	Engages in intellectual play; enjoys puns, play on words, language games.
Visualizes spatially, can create visual images of problems.	Prefers science-related classes and careers.	Likes to do independent study and research in areas of interest.	Enjoys the processes of research and investigating for their own sake.

(Continued)

Table 2.2 (Continued)

Mathematics	Science	English	Humanities
Develops unique associations, uses original methods for solutions.	Persistent, sticks with investigations in spite of difficulties or problems, has high level of energy.	Motivated to write even when writing is not assigned; writes stories, poems, or plays; keeps a journal or diary.	Recalls details about social science topics, makes unusual connections.
Sometimes solves problems intuitively, then cannot always explain why the solution is correct.	Knows a lot of science information.	Sees relationship between literature and other art forms.	Interested in social themes, complex public issues, explanations, and theories of causation.
Recalls relevant information or concepts in solving problems, recognizes the critical elements.	Skilful in using lab equipment, able to improvise for experiments.	Uses words effectively in writing descriptions and communicating emotions.	Curious about many things, 'goes off on tangents'.

frequently), or 4 (always or almost always) based on the observed frequency. DK is used for when teachers 'don't know' or haven't observed the behaviour.

Administering behaviour checklists

There are several ways checklists and rating scales such as the Purdue examples can be used. Firstly, schools could use an online survey tool to develop an electronic version to be shared with teachers. Placing this in a central online location creates easy access for teachers to complete at any time. Clear instructions should be placed at the top reminding teachers of how to complete the scale or checklist. For rating scales, schools might determine scores that form cut points. For checklists, counts of the number of behaviours exhibited can be used to inform the next steps. Most checklists and scales will have instructions about what to do with the data once you have it.

Scales and checklists can also be used for professional learning and provide teachers with characteristics they can look for when working with their class. For example, a Year 7 Maths team could use some of their meeting time during Term 1 to review the behaviours of high-potential mathematicians and discuss this in the context of their own class. Given the time of year, they are still getting to know students and learn about their abilities and potential. Being able to link observed behaviours to high-potential characteristics can give teachers a better idea of how to cater for these learners.

Something to consider before sending out the first link or paper checklist is what will happen with the completed forms. From experience, being inundated with forms can become very overwhelming! Who collects the forms will be determined by the purpose of completing the checklists. If it is for a withdrawal programme, there may be a coordinator or teacher(s) that have responsibility for this. If it is for a classroom teacher's own information, then they might keep it with their class records and discuss results with their teaching team. In one school, two teachers were responsible for the administration and collection of the forms as the purpose was to identify students for withdrawal programmes they were running. Rather than store the forms in a locked cabinet or password protected network drive, the information was uploaded and attached to the student's online learning information record. This way, other teachers who worked with the student could benefit from the insights.

Parents as early identifiers

One group of people that do know a learner well is parents. Parents can be an underused resource with concern they will be biased, overstating what their child can do. Unfortunately, this has several consequences including parents being reluctant to advocate for their child to avoid being 'pushy' and school's not valuing the insights parents can offer and excluding them in the process. For the teachers, reflect on the conversations you've had during parent-teacher interviews. There are often stark differences in the child's behaviours at school compared to what parents experienced at home. At school, the day is structured around lessons of set durations, with content that is often determined and shaped by the teacher to meet the requirements of the mandated curriculum. But what if this environment and the topics being taught weren't of interest to the learner? What if the learner's interests lay in geology and they spent weekends as part of a geology club, or completing online courses? Through using the parent form, I learnt a lot about students that I might otherwise have never found out, such as a child in Year 2 who learnt binary at the dinner table one night. Checklists like the Sayler's parent checklist[12] (readily available online) provide parents with a selection of statements that are linked to characteristics of gifted and talented learners. After providing an indication of how much they agree or disagree with the statement, there is space for personal examples to be recorded. This is the most valuable part of this form as a picture of the learner beyond school constraints is brought to light. A couple of suggestions if you decide to use this a part of your identification battery:

- Provide an online version using one of the online form apps. This saves time printing, sending, chasing returned forms, and storage of completed forms. Also means there is a repository so doubling-up on forms in successive years is avoided.
- *Communicate with parents* about the purpose of the form. The biggest concern raised by teachers and schools when proposing the use of this tool is that parents will make assumptions about what happens next. In one school, we changed the title to reflect it was 'investigative' and that completion of the questionnaire did not guarantee selection into specialized gifted provisions within the school. A sample letter used with parents is in Box 2.3.

Box 2.3 Sample parent letter

Dear Parents

Your child's class teacher is investigating whether or not your child may be eligible to enter our Enrichment program, which offers a range of activities to students who are achieving at, or have the potential to achieve at, a level **significantly** above that expected of their age group.

In order to develop a full sense of your child, we are asking that you complete the attached checklist and return to your child's class teacher at your earliest convenience.

Please note that this process is very involved and uses a range of valid and fair data in the selection process. Completion of this checklist does not automatically assume entry into the program.

If you would like to discuss this matter further, please contact me at school on Monday or Tuesday, or via the school email address.

- Consider your audience. Families for whom English is not their first language may not be able to describe in great detail the scope of their experiences. If feasible, you may consider having questions translated into the appropriate language and allowing them to respond in their first language and then translating back to English.

As discussed above, consider where these completed surveys will be stored, and who will have access to it. As with the teacher checklist, experience has shown that the information in these surveys is valuable for teachers working with the student. Having this information in a location that allows appropriate personnel access is worth considering. This may be determined by the policies and systems at the local school level.

Student self-nomination works in a similar way to the parent form. Instead of statements, students respond to questions that are designed to tap into behavioural characteristics of gifted and talented learners. Questions such as 'What do you like to do in your spare time?' and 'Who would you most like to meet?' provide a window into aspects of a student's life and interests that may not be demonstrated at school. Alternatively, students may be asked to write an autobiography, guided by questions reflecting on greatest success/failure, events and/or people that have shaped their lives.

How do you know what to use?

Some jurisdictions have very clear guidelines and criteria for identifying gifted and talented students. A recent review of Australia's education jurisdictions identified 14 different criteria in policy documents across the nation (see Box 2.4)[13]. The location of a school will play a role in determining the strategies used. For example, in Victoria, there are recommended criteria for the strategies used such as having multiple criteria, including stakeholders and having a combination of objective and subjective measures. In New South Wales and South Australia, these are mandatory. Regardless of whether the criteria are mandatory, suggested, or not mentioned, they are important considerations to keep in mind when determining how you will identify gifted and talented students in your setting.

Box 2.4 Criteria used in Australian educational jurisdictions' policy

1. School-wide approach
2. Multiple criteria
3. Inclusive
4. Dynamic and continuous
5. Culturally fair
6. Include all 'domains' and 'fields'
7. Recognize degrees of giftedness and talent
8. Link to differentiation
9. Allow for early identification
10. Be inclusive of stakeholders
11. Specialized or flexible for minority groups
12. A combination of subjective and objective strategies
13. Reliable
14. Valid

(Adapted from Slater, E. (2018). The identification of gifted children in Australia: The importance of policy. *TalentEd*, 30, 1–16)

How to make sure your practice is defensible, equitable, and fair?

In the previous chapter, Table 1.4 illustrates how each of the theories would shape the identification practices used within schools. The principles and definitions underpinning the theory should determine the approach the school takes to identify and select students who will participate in specialized programs. Figure 2.1 illustrates what this might look like for the Differentiating Model of Gifts and Talents (DMGT) and the Active Concerned Citizenship and Ethical Leadership (ACCEL) model. There is no right or wrong choice when determining which model you work with, although as stated, the model that guides your practice may be influenced by your relevant education department. Nor is there any reason why you can't use multiple models to shape the identification and programming practices in your context. You may wish to establish a domain-specific talent development program in Mathematics. Using the DMGT, you determine that students who fall within the 90th percentile on an achievement test are considered the target group. This group may then form a regular withdrawal program where systematic development

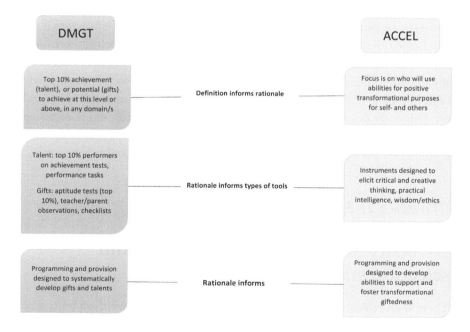

Figure 2.1 Comparison of how theories shape practice

of mathematical skills and understandings takes place. As well as offering a Maths program, your team determines that the focus of the ACCEL model is highly valued, and you establish a set of materials that will identify students for a withdrawal programme designed to develop critical and creative thinking, practical intelligence, and wisdom and ethics. This is not a cut and dry 'top 10%' rule that can be applied. Rather, the team will need to look at responses and perhaps a range of other tools (e.g., self-nomination, application form) to determine who might be best suited for that specific program.

Once these decisions have been determined and agreed upon, it is useful to represent this process in a flow chart. A flow chart demonstrates clearly, to all stakeholders, the how and why of identification. See Appendix A for an example of how two flowcharts, based on the DMGT, have been developed and used in schools.

What about twice-exceptional students?

Twice-exceptional students, also referred to as 2e, are learners who are gifted and have a disability[14]. The form of disability may be physical or sensory (e.g., hearing impairment), developmental (e.g., ADHD or ASD), learning (e.g., dyslexia), or psychosocial (e.g., anxiety). Often, the focus of educators is on the disability, rather than the ability of the learner. For 2e students, there must be an absolute focus on ensuring conditions allow them to demonstrate their abilities and potential. For example, a learner with ASD who fails to complete tasks in class is not lazy. Rather, they probably need support in planning and breaking tasks down. They may need more time for planning and completing the work than others. It is our responsibility to make sure they have the conditions and opportunities to demonstrate their high ability or high potential.

Taking it further

Diversity and bias in identification and selection strategies

There is an ethical aspect to the selection and identification of students who receive additional programming outside of normal classroom teaching (e.g., withdrawal programs, participation in competitions). For every student that is invited to take part in a program or experience, there are many who are left out. This is often a criticism about Gifted Education or extension and enrichment programs in schools.

When I have asked teachers to nominate high ability or gifted students, they often mention the names of students who do well on tests and schoolwork, are generally well-behaved in class, are independent in their learning, motivated, and can be depended on for giving the correct answer during class discussions, i.e., 'the good student'. The perception of what 'giftedness' or high potential/ability looks like is varied and often narrow, exacerbated by limited coverage in initial teacher education courses[15] and subsequent teacher professional learning. Students have been dismissed due to disruptive behaviours, lack of focus, lack of motivation, or minimum productivity. A teacher commented to me once that a child didn't deserve to attend a withdrawal program because she wasn't completing enough class work. As it turned out, this child had dysgraphia and writing was hard work for her, but she was a voracious reader and could tell an amazing story.

There are a number of factors that will influence what teachers look for in high-ability/potential students and these will be shaped by the teachers' beliefs, expectations, stereotypes, and biases[16]. A useful activity to do either on your own or with colleagues is to answer the question, 'what does a high-ability student "look" like?' What do they say and do? What are the implicit criteria you have for whether you deem someone to be high potential? What does this look like in children compared to adults? How you respond is likely to be how you view the children in your class and shape your responses and actions. These responses may be unintentionally biased towards one group or type of learner, for example recognizing reading strengths more so than other areas of strength[17]. This is where the teacher checklists are particularly useful to encourage a broader view of how high potential may present.

I believe that mainstream education places too great an emphasis on the structured learning, response and assessment methods/processes. Has consideration been given to the importance of aural learning and the ability to comprehend and articulate this understanding through storytelling without the need for writing an answer being the only method for assessment? Our people passed on knowledge aurally, captured events through art and celebrated through dance and song, which are not necessarily reflected in a student's ability to be classified as gifted. They may have a nice voice or paint well, but these are not necessarily valued until later years (when the child could have become disengaged from school or continuing their education). Additionally, do the continuous confines of a classroom inhibit the ability of the student?

– Michael (Barkindji and Wemba-Wemba man)

When there is a clearly defined and communicated rationale behind decisions, and a shared understanding of how high potential and talent is defined, there is greater understanding and wider acceptance of the programme in general. If selection of top performers is the preferred model, then situating this within a rationale and purpose (i.e., talent development) will make it easier to make and defend decisions. However, an important consideration when using only achievement data, or any assessment tool used for identification and selection, is measurement bias.

Bias in assessments refers to fairness, and in this context, how the tools used in the identification process may be unfair for some students leading to exclusion or lack of consideration. A well-known example is the link between achievement and family socio-economic status (SES), with results from both the National Assessment Program – Literacy and Numeracy (NAPLAN) [18] and the Australian Tertiary Admission Rank (ATAR) [19] showing high performance linked to higher SES that declines with lower SES. In addition to SES, factors such as language and cultural background, religion, disability, health, gender, and neurodivergence may also lead to assessments or tools being unfair to diverse students. Consider the following scenarios and then reflect on the discussion provided.

Scenario 1: A primary school is establishing an withdrawal programme for its gifted and talented students. The number of students that can be involved is limited given the resources of the school. The team responsible for this has determined that they would like to include parents of children nominated by teachers as being suitable for the program to inform their decisions. The school sends out a link to an electronic version of the Sayler parent checklist they created using Google Forms, with an explanation as to why they are being asked to complete it. A due date is provided, and the team reviews the responses together. They notice that many of the parents have provided lots of anecdotes and written extensively about their child.

The team is easily able to recognize the needs of these students and decide to invite them into the program. But there are others who have only a sentence or two for some questions, and others are left blank. All the team has to go on is the rating parents have provided. As a result, given the lack of information, the team determines to exclude these children for now.

Scenario 2: A secondary school relies on achievement tests alone to determine who is offered a place in their high-potential programme. The school has an established practice where all students attending their Year 7 Orientation Day sit an achievement test as a way of learning more about their learning needs. This data is used to determine who will be offered a place, with potential participants needing to be in the top 10%, if not higher, depending on numbers each year. Students with scores less than 90% are not considered.

Scenario 3: A secondary school is establishing a withdrawal programme to develop the abilities of high-potential students in Mathematics. Teachers are asked to look at their testing data and put forward the names of any students they think will benefit. Teachers review their mark books and highlight students who score consistently high (above 90%) on all assessments.

Scenario 1 discussion

One argument supporting the team's decision might be that the families had an opportunity to provide the information, and they based their decision on the information they had. The form was written in, and required responses, in English. The form was sent to families with a language background other than English with low levels of proficiency or a level of proficiency that didn't allow them to easily respond to the questions describing their child. Using this instrument in this way creates bias as it did not adequately allow parents to share their knowledge of their child in the same way as parents for whom English is their first language or who are highly proficient in English.

Scenario 2 discussion

Not everyone performs well under test conditions. Add an Orientation Day to that and it can become a mix of nerves, anticipation, overwhelm, stress, and anxiety. For high-potential neurodivergent students who may require more time to complete tests, or students with anxiety, the results from a test in the context of an Orientation Day may not be reliable. The school introduces an ongoing process of identification where teachers, students, and parents can nominate to be included in the programme and use other tools to identify students who may suffer test anxiety.

Scenario 3 discussion

Whilst looking for consistently high performance in Maths assessment as an indicator of high Maths ability, the focus on scores (often recorded as percentages) loses nuance. In each of the assessments, there is a section of worded problems using technical language. An EAL (English as an Additional Language) student in the class always does really well in any section using equations and symbols, but the worded problems are difficult for them to understand. As such, their overall mark gets dragged down and they often score in the 80–89% range.

Each of the scenarios describes ways in which tools used for identification may have some bias for some students and their families. There are some easy solutions for each, but ultimately making sure a variety of tools are used is key, both objective and subjective. Being mindful of how tools may disadvantage some students is critical, particularly for those from disadvantaged backgrounds. Students can only demonstrate what they can do or have the potential to do when given an opportunity to do so. An absence of evidence does not automatically mean an absence of potential.

Summary

This chapter discussed the difference between identification and selection and introduced several subjective and objective tools that can be used. When a wide range of tools and strategies are used to identify student learning needs, it adds rigour to the process and increases the likelihood of capturing diverse learners. Furthermore, when we can demonstrate to the school community that multiple approaches are used, there is a greater level of trust and appreciation that the process is well-considered. Keep in mind that the information you collect throughout your process needs to be treated with the same care as all student data. Privacy and confidentiality need to be respected and maintained. Students and parents must be informed about how the data will be used, stored, and shared.

An important and final note is to recognize that identification isn't just for those who offer separate or additional provisions such as withdrawal programmes, etc. The use of checklists and other subjective measures may help identify high-potential learning needs that have otherwise gone unnoticed or be misrepresented as simply problematic behaviour. Chapter 5 outlines six profiles and gifted, talented, and creative learners that provides additional perspectives on the different types of high-potential learners.

Key points to take away when it comes to identifying high-potential students in your school:

1. Cast a wide net, and never stop fishing. Remain vigilant and empower all teachers to be on the lookout for students demonstrating high-potential behaviours
2. Use a variety of identification tools and be aware of how the selected tools may be unfair to some students. Be flexible in how you adapt these to get the information you need
3. Always include parents and students in the process
4. Be clear about the rationale behind your identification and selection processes. What is the purpose for identification, selection, and ultimate programming?

Chapter Reflection

Part a: for everyone

1. What advice would you give your school about how to identify high-ability, high-potential learners? Create an identification process flow chart that communicates how you do this in practice.
2. Think of someone you know that you believe to be high ability/ high potential (friend, student, colleague, family member). What do you base that belief on? What tools would confirm that, or help others learn about their capabilities?

Part b: for those with an existing high ability/enrichment program

1. What are your current identification practices based on? Write in one sentence the rationale guiding your practices.

2. Conduct an audit of the tools and strategies (use Table 2.1 to help you). How transparent are these practices? Who knows about them and how do you use them?
3. Identify any next steps for your current practice based on any insights from this chapter.

Notes

1 Fatih, K. (2013). The role of peer nomination forms in the identification of lower elementary gifted and talented students. *Educational Research and Reviews*, *8*(24), 2260–2269.
2 https://paa.com.au/product/grs/#:~:text=The%20Gifted%20Rating%20 Scales%20are,0%20and%206%3A11%20years
3 https://www.acer.org/au/hast-primary
4 https://www.pearsonclinical.com.au/store/auassessments/en/Store/Professional-Assessments/Cognition-%26-Neuro/Raven%27s-2/p/P100010205.html
5 https://www.pearsonassessments.com/store/usassessments/en/Store/ Professional-Assessments/Cognition-%26-Neuro/Gifted-%26-Talented/Wechsler-Intelligence-Scale-for-Children-%7C-Fifth-Edition-/p/100000771.html
6 wpspublish.com/catalogsearch/result/?q=stanford
7 Pfeiffer, S. I., & Jarosewich, T. (2007). The Gifted Rating Scales-School Form:An analysis of the standardization sample based on age, gender, race, and diagnostic efficiency. *Gifted Child Quarterly*, *51*(1), 39–50. https://doi. org/10.1177/0016986206296658
8 Li, H., Lee, D., Pfeiffer, S. I., Kamata, A., Kumtepe, A. T., & Rosado, J. (2009). Measurement invariance of the Gifted Rating Scales—School Form across five cultural groups. *School Psychology Quarterly*, *24*(3), 186.
9 Merrick, C., & Targett, R. (2004) Gifted and talented education professional development package for teachers: Module 2 Primary. https://www.unsw.edu.au/ content/dam/images/photos/campus/kensington/2021-06-gerric-documents/ 2021-06-gerric-Module2_primary.pdf
10 Feldhusen, J. F., Hoover, S. M., & Sayler, M. F. (1990). Purdue Academic Rating Scales. In *Identifying and educating gifted students at the secondary level* (pp. 5–11).
11 Ibid.
12 Sayler, M. (n.d.). Gifted and talented checklist for parents: Things my child has done. University of North Texas.
13 Slater, E. (2018). The identification of gifted children in Australia: The importance of policy. *TalentEd*, *30*(2018), 1–16.

14 Foley-Nicpon, M., Assouline, S. G., & Colangelo, N. (2013). Twice-Exceptional Learners:Who Needs to Know What? *Gifted Child Quarterly, 57*(3), 169–180. https://doi.org/10.1177/0016986213490021 ley-Nicpon, M., Assouline, S. G., & Colangelo, N. (2013). Twice-Exceptional Learners:Who Needs to Know What? *Gifted Child Quarterly, 57*(3), 169–180. https://doi.org/10.1177/0016986213490021

15 Plunkett, M., & Kronborg, L. (2021). Teaching gifted education to pre-service teachers: Lessons learned. In S. Smith (Ed.), *Handbook of giftedness and talent development in the Asia-Pacific*, (pp. 1409-1430).

16 Siegle, D., Moore, M., Mann, R. L., & Wilson, H. E. (2010). Factors that influence in-service and preservice teachers' nominations of students for gifted and talented programs. *Journal for the Education of the Gifted, 33*(3), 337–360.

17 Hodge, K. A., & Kemp, C. R. (2006). Recognition of giftedness in the early years of school: Perspectives of teachers, parents, and children. Ibid., *30*(2), 164–204.

18 Forgasz, H., & Leder, G. (2020). The NAPLAN numeracy test: do school type and socio-economic background make a difference? *Mathematics Education Research Journal*, 1–14.

19 Manny, A. (2020). *Socio-economic status and the ATAR*. University Admissions Centre. https://www.uac.edu.au/assets/documents/atar/SES-and-the-ATAR-report.pdf

References

Gross, M.U.M. (2004). Module one: Understanding Giftedness (Primary). Professional development package for teachers: Gifted education professional development package. DEST (Department of Education, Science and Training) & GERRIC. Retrieved from https://www.unsw.edu.au/content/dam/images/photos/campus/kensington/2021-06-gerric-documents/2021-06-gerric-module1-primary.pdf

Rimm, S. B., Siegle, D., & Davis, G. A. (2018). *Education of the gifted and talented*. Pearson.

APPENDIX A: IDENTIFICATION PROCESS FLOW CHARTS

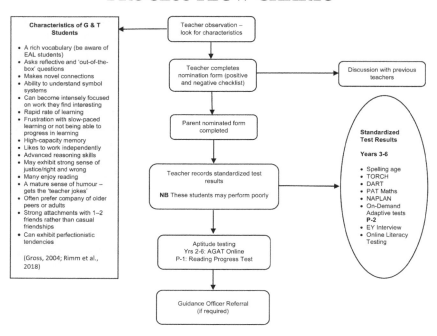

Figure A.1 Identification process flow chart examples: Gifted

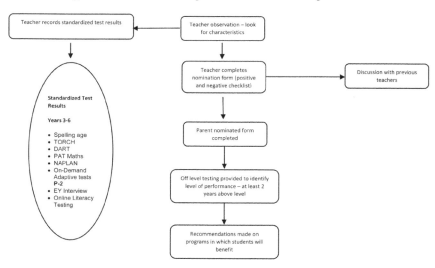

Figure A.2 Identification process flow chart example: Talented

3 | Provision, Curriculum, and Pedagogies

BACK TO BASICS

There are multiple provisions that can be used when working with gifted students. These include within-class programs and strategies and activities beyond the classroom such as mentoring or collaborating with outside agencies. A comprehensive range of provisions, including types of acceleration, are described with examples provided for each. Curriculum adjustments to learning environment, product, process, and content are discussed. Types of assessment and their utility for this cohort of students are introduced, with an emphasis on formative assessment. Underachievement amongst this cohort of students, along with some of the contributing factors and ways in which underachieving students can be supported are discussed.

TAKING IT FURTHER

This section will focus on design thinking and student co-created teaching and learning and the ways they can be used with gifted students.

> I always get frustrated by 'box-ticking' in all different areas. Even when I'm more than capable with the material and can go ahead on my own, I still have to do all the regular class work
>
> – Rowan (Year 10)

DOI: 10.4324/9781003267973-3

Teaching is a hard job. Each day, teachers face a class full of students, all with individual learning needs, interests, personalities, strengths, and weaknesses. How do we ensure all students can thrive in their learning? Differentiation? Have you ever noticed how many books there are about differentiation? Time is precious, and if we can pick up a book that has a clear 'how-to' that will translate easily and somewhat effortlessly into our classrooms, then please take my money! Unfortunately, I don't think there is a quick-fix that can be found in these books.

I learned that to provide appropriate learning opportunities for my students, I needed to make modifications in my teaching (and buy fewer books with pre-prepared units). Making modifications to lessons to cater for students happens all the time in classrooms, particularly in primary settings. However, these modifications largely occur based on a deficit model. The focus is on what students cannot yet do or have not yet achieved, usually in terms of curriculum outcomes and standards based on year level. A deficit perspective can be detrimental to students who have already acquired the required skills, understandings, or knowledge.

A developmental perspective provides us with a different lens focusing on growth. This perspective asks us to consider: what does the student already know; and what is the student ready to learn next?[1] It is important to consider your own views and the lens you apply regarding learning, teaching, and assessment. The curriculum you work with may influence whether you adopt a deficit or developmental approach. The national Australian Curriculum is an age-based standards-referenced framework where achievement standards are linked to year levels[2]. Working within frameworks such as this, where standards are linked to levels, may focus efforts on ensuring students *meet* these standards. But what if they are already *exceeding* these? Conversely, the structure of Victorian Curriculum is based on levels of learning, rather than year levels, as the framework is seen as a developmental continuum[3].

A developmental perspective provides the foundation for achieving the goal of 'delivering at least one year's growth in learning for every student every year'[4] (p. 12). Unfortunately, in Australian schools, the current focus is more on achievement at a point in time, rather than on the progress learners are making[5]. It should be noted that progress is not a synonym for achievement. Progress is about the value-add, not about reaching an achievement band.

What does this mean in terms of high-ability students? It means that there will be no silver bullet resource that will help us differentiate. It means we need to start with our own practice and identify ways we can

1. determine what these learners already know and can do
2. determine what they need to, or want to, learn next
3. select appropriate interventions, or teaching strategies, to help them get there.

These steps will be discussed in further detail with some practical strategies to use with your learners. Some of these strategies can be implemented in classrooms straightaway, others require greater consideration.

Determine what these learners already know and can do

Let us skip things we already understand. If you replace the easy work instead of adding to it, you allow a lot of people to access extension who wouldn't have the time or energy to do it otherwise. Remember, a high IQ doesn't give you more hours in a day!

– Rowan (Year 10)

By identifying what learners already know and can do, we can eliminate putting students in learning environments that lead to boredom and frustration and free up time for them to learn. To identify what learners already know and can do, we need to assess. All teachers are familiar with formative assessment or assessment for learning. However, how well this is understood and done is variable. A useful definition of formative assessment[6] is:

An assessment functions formatively to the extent that evidence about student achievement is elicited, interpreted, and used by teachers, learners or their peers to make decisions about the next steps in instruction that are likely to be better, or better founded, than the decisions they would have made in the absence of that evidence.

(p. 48)

Formative assessment is about evidence of student learning and using that evidence to inform what happens next. There are a multitude of strategies for eliciting the skills and knowledge students already have, both before and during teaching a unit or topic. Students need to have **opportunities,** planned or unplanned, to demonstrate their current level of skills and understanding, and these opportunities should be available to everyone, not just those identified as gifted and talented. You may gain insight into students who may be dumbing down, or compliant and 'going with the flow' of the classroom, who learn the content quickly, or who may tune out most lessons and fail to get much, if anything, done.

There needs to be opportunities for students to show what they know prior to beginning a new topic or unit. When planning how to elicit this evidence, consider the diversity in your class and provide different ways and formats of assessment (see the discussion of bias in Chapter 2). Evidence can be in the form of what they do, say, make, and write. For example, in Mathematics, do students need to complete a quiz or a test at the beginning of a unit? How else might they demonstrate their understandings? Students could be offered an opportunity to complete the hardest five problems first. If they can complete these, you could probably safely assume they do not need to spend time on the foundational concepts. When introducing a Science or Humanities and Social Sciences (HASS) topic, learners could complete a concept map demonstrating their understanding of key concepts and the relationships between these. If using pre-tests or quizzes, use off-level tests, where the ceiling can be removed or raised – we don't learn much to assist our teaching when learners get everything correct.

> I was often eager to learn more than what was being taught...I thought many teachers were reluctant to teach me more than what was necessary
> – Ella (Year 11)

The idea of students completing different work or skipping the 'fundamentals' can be challenging for teachers. There can be a perception that students need to complete the planned topic material first, before moving onto concepts and understandings that will enable them to learn something new. Sometimes this is attached to a sense of what is fair, or what other students may perceive as being unfair. This is where offering the opportunity for all students to demonstrate mastery of the intended learning is useful. For those who do, we have just freed up valuable time to extend the learning or introduce new ideas. If all students can complete the hardest problems, then it's to review what needs to be taught.

Table 3.1 provides a list of different strategies that could be used to assess what the learner is ready to learn next.

Table 3.1 Formative assessment strategies

Concept maps	K-W-L charts
Venn diagrams	Student reflections
Flow charts	Question shells
Hands-on activities	Hot-seat questioning
Think-alouds	All student response systems
Draw a diagram	Exit pass
Diagnostic questions	Mini whiteboards
Discussion questions	Student self-assessment
Hardest problems first	Observations
Off-level questions/quiz	

Determine what they need to, or want to, learn next

A core element of adopting a developmental approach to teaching and assessment is the idea that the constructs we teach can be broken down into observable behaviours in the form of a learning progression. If we think of topics or units that we teach, e.g., fractions, there is a progression of learning that begins with recognizing that a whole can be broken down into parts leading to performing operations with fractional indices. This is a big leap and of course there are many ideas and concepts that need to be introduced to enable this development to occur.

In practice, however, what I often experienced was working with *year-level*-based curriculum and resources. Scope and sequence charts outlined the understandings we were to teach and seemed to create a boundary around what was to be taught. But if we want students to be able to achieve at least one year's growth throughout the academic year, rather than considering the year-level-specific learning outcomes, wouldn't we be better off thinking about what they are ready to learn next, regardless of the level at which it is described in a curriculum document?

Ask gifted/talented/high-ability students (and their parents), if the students want more challenges at school (before offering them)

– Sally (parent)

An argument against moving students forward is the implications for next year's teacher. What happens if you teach the Level 5 and Level 6 content in Year 4? What does the Year 6 teacher teach? My question is, what happens if you don't? As teachers, we are often the gatekeepers of the ideas and understandings our students have access to. Of course, they can, and sometimes do, go beyond what is delivered during school hours. This may be with external tutors, or using online resources, such as Kahn Academy. But given they have dedicated time to learning, each day, for 40 weeks each year, wouldn't that time be better served in providing opportunities to continue developing their understandings and facilitating progress?

> I enjoy learning the most when the topics are both interesting and challenging. Also, if it is something which is not usually covered in the school curriculum, as this gives me the opportunity to learn something new which I may not have had the chance to do otherwise.
>
> – Synthia (Year 11)

An alternative to making continuous progress in the area of study is to provide students with opportunities to explore content beyond the curriculum. This may be related to the area of learning, or it may be a new area altogether. For example, if the Maths focus is geometry, students could explore polyhedra, or combine concepts such as networks and polyhedra as the basis of an investigation using balloon modelling!

> Identify they are bright!…Once identified, meet with the parents and the child and work through based on the child's personality, the best way to logistically provide additional work. For our daughter, it needed to be done in a subtle manner and driven by the teacher, not our daughter, given her personality
>
> – Jodie (parent)

The best strategy to determine the way forward in addressing what the learner needs, or wants to learn next, is to discuss this with the learner and their family. Regardless of age, the learner should have some input into what they are learning next once mastery has been demonstrated. As teachers, we cannot presume to always know what is appropriate as we are not always privy to the experiences of the learner outside of the school setting. Conversations help identify interests and may point us in the right direction of suggesting an area that the student is not yet aware and appropriate ways of providing these opportunities.

Select appropriate interventions, or teaching strategies, to help them get there

Acceleration: the most effective invention

There are several strategies teachers can use to assist in providing appropriate learning opportunities for high-ability students. Outlined in Table 3.2[7, 8] is a selection of acceleration strategies and the effect that each of these strategies has in terms of the growth that occurs, or the practical significance of the strategy. Acceleration refers to the advanced rate students move through the curriculum as per their ability, rather than being lock-stepped according to age and grade level[9]. Acceleration strategies can be described as subject/content-based or grade-based. Grade-based acceleration strategies will typically shorten the amount of time spent in school, such as skipping a year or grade level, or starting school early (although the same amount of time may be spent at school).

Decisions about acceleration need to be made with the student and their family. They are not decisions to be made without their input nor their consent. What works for one student may not work for another, and if the student is not comfortable with the approach, that needs to be respected. Communication is key when determining the best approach for each learner. That way, families and students know what to expect, not just in the immediate context, but in the years that follow.

Curriculum compacting: A differentiation strategy

Curriculum compacting is a strategy whereby content that is already mastered by students is eliminated from further instruction, practice, or drill. Research has shown that primary-aged students can skip 50–75% of the year-level curriculum and not compromise their mastery of the content[10]. This provides the learner with a lot of time that can now be used in any number of ways. It may be to extend their learning in the area of study, or the time

Table 3.2 Acceleration strategies, descriptions, and effects

Strategy	Description/example	Effect size
Compacted curriculum	Time saved from eliminating/ reduced content is used for more advanced content or enrichment	Academic: slight Social: moderate Psychological: slight
Online courses	May be formal or informal	Academic: strong Social: Psychological: moderate
Early access to university units	Complete a university-accredited unit while in Year 11 or 12	No studies reported
Grade skipping	Learners bypass one or two years	Academic: strong Social: moderate Psychological: moderate
Independent study	Students are provided a structure for in-depth study of a topic of interest during the school day	No studies reported
Individualized acceleration	Students work at their own pace through continuous progress content and skill areas	Academic: slight Social: Moderate Psychological: Moderate
Mentorship/ coaching	Placement with a content expert to extend learning in the content area	Academic: slight Social: strong Psychological: slight
Single-subject acceleration	Students bypass the usual progress in ONE subject, progressing normally in others	Academic: moderate Psychological: moderate
Telescoping curriculum	Instruction is provided that entails less time than is normal, e.g., One year in 6 months. Always results in advanced grade placement	

could be used to introduce and expose learners to new concepts and ideas within the domain. This approach relies on the use of formative assessment or any other evidence of mastery (e.g., previous reports) to determine what can be eliminated. Mastery does not require 100% accuracy all the time. Rather, the benchmark should be set at 80% accuracy. Teachers are often concerned about gaps in student knowledge, and this is a reasonable concern. However, given the rate at which high-ability students learn, it usually will only take one or two exposures to the missing skill or concept for the student to have filled the gap.

There are five key steps when compacting the curriculum[11]:

1. Determine what is to be learned by all students (e.g., adding and subtracting fractions).
2. Determine who already knows this through pre-testing of the whole class, or by offering an opportunity for those who feel they know the content to demonstrate their mastery.
3. Plan alternative pathways for those students who have demonstrated mastery or who will likely master the content quickly. This may be through accelerating the content and pace for those who will learn it quickly, teaching the next level of understandings (in the learning progression), or it might be an opportunity for the learner to explore something new. If exploring something new, this can be shaped by the learner in negotiation with the teacher.
4. Eliminate any drill or practice of the mastered skill or understanding and avoid providing 'more of the same' as a way of keeping the student working.
5. Maintain a record of the compacting activities and share this with families as per school-based reporting and communication procedures.

Providing students with **independent study** is one way of using the time that is now available. Negotiating with the learner about what will be studied and providing a scaffold and check-points will set them up for success and not leave them floundering. Of course, this may not be an appropriate strategy for all students. Working independently requires motivation, organization, and commitment to be productive and drive their own learning. The amount of support and structure needed will vary from student to student. It's important to remember that just because a learner is gifted, or has high ability, it does not mean they will be 'model' students, with unwavering motivation, advanced organizational skills, or know how to proceed on the project at hand. While there are no reported effect sizes for this approach, the comments from students, primary and secondary, indicate that this is a valued strategy that enables them to tap into and extend their curiosity about a range of ideas and interests.

> I am ok to continue on with independent learning and to read ahead while the class is learning about something else but it is generally helpful to have a tiny bit of direction on this so I know that I am heading in the right direction. For example, knowing what future topics are, having an indication on relevant textbook chapters etc.
>
> – Synthia (Year 11)

Questions to ask:

- Do I know what the learner is interested in learning about?
- What areas might they be interested in, but not yet exposed to?
- What level of scaffolding and structure does the student need to experience success?
- What are the expectations of this study? Have these been negotiated and communicated clearly with the student and their family?

Individualized acceleration allows the student to keep learning, to make continuous progress on the content and skill areas. There is a slight academic effect reported for this strategy, but the social and psychological effects are moderate. Removing the ceiling of what can be 'learned' within a unit based on age and stage facilitates growth and may prevent issues of underachievement, reticence, lowered academic self-esteem, and social or behavioural maladjustments[7]. For teachers, it means we need to know what comes next in the learning progression and ensure we can provide the learner with access to the advanced content and skills. Using online resources or online courses may be one way of providing this.

Questions to ask:

- Do I know what to teach next? If not, where can I find out?
- Is there any expertise in the school?
- For primary teachers – how might the local secondary school be able to help?
- What online resources could I use?
- How can this progress be assessed and reported within the school's current assessment and reporting systems?

Single-subject acceleration is similar to individualized acceleration; however, it may be that rather than basing the continuous progress on a unit at a time, the determination is made that the content and skills at a higher year level are consistently more appropriate. Organizationally, this may mean the student attends a different class for that particular subject, and then returns to their usual class for everything else. Ideally, school structures need to be in place where subjects are taught at the same time so that learning in other areas is not missed. This is one strategy that requires planning, discussions, and review as a school and with the family. The student needs to feel comfortable moving to another, usually older, class for subject acceleration. There needs to be a plan in place for what happens the following year. If in primary school, what happens when they are in Year Six, typically their last year before moving into secondary. How will their learning be catered for then? There are solutions to these problems, and the key is knowing in advance what the trajectory will look like in two, three, or four years' time. The planning can be presented to the family and the learner so they can make an informed decision about how to proceed. Of course, things may change and deviate from the plan along the way. It may be that a single-year-level acceleration isn't enough. Scheduling review and check-in times is necessary to monitor how well the acceleration is going. This includes checking in with the teaching staff, parents, and the learner.

Questions to ask:

- Is subject acceleration a suitable strategy for this student? Is the student open to it? Is the family on board? Does the school leadership support this strategy? Is there a suitable class for this learner to accelerate?
- Who will be responsible for assessment and reporting on learner progress in this subject?
- How will teachers communicate? How often? What mode?
- When will we check in with the family?
- How will we know if the subject acceleration is working? What does success look like?
- What happens next year? And the year after that? What is the long-term pathway?

Grade skipping

This is often the most confronting strategy when exploring options for high-ability students. Common objections from teachers are based on social or emotional implications – the student is too young, too immature, and won't have any friends.

Grade skipping is as the name suggests: students skip a year level or grade ahead of their chronological-age classmates. This can occur at any time during the school year but makes sense if it can be planned for the start of the year for an easier transition for the student. Planning for the transition is key and ensuring the student will manage the skip is vital (e.g., emotionally, socially). This strategy requires consideration of the transition process as well as how the student is supported post-transition. It is helpful to establish a transition plan that details the ways in which the academic, social, and emotional needs of the learner will be monitored and supported. A staff member needs to take responsibility of overseeing the transition and being the key contact for other staff, parents, and most importantly, the learner, in the absence of a Gifted Education specialist in the school, this could be a well-being teacher or leader, year-level coordinator, or a learning support teacher. This strategy must have student buy-in. They must want to skip a grade and there should be open and frank conversations with the student so they know the benefits and drawbacks of this acceleration. A case study is described in Box 3.1 detailing the grade-skipping process for a student skipping from Year 5 to

Box 3.1 Case study: Grade skipping

A Year 5 primary school aged student, Sarah, was identified as being academically advanced. She was attending a K-12 school, and received a scholarship for the final two years of her primary education. Sarah was attending a weekly withdrawal program delivered by a Gifted Education specialist teacher and her class teacher was proactive in making modifications for Sarah on a daily basis. Sarah's main academic strength was in Mathematics, although she was an all-rounder. The Gifted Education teacher identified several acceleration pathways available to Sarah and provided a description of each option highlighting what it meant for Sarah by considering the dimensions of acceleration, i.e., salience, peers, pacing, access, and timing.

Sarah and her parents used this document to discuss the options as a family. A follow-up meeting occurred with the principal, Sarah, her parents, and the Gifted Education teacher where additional questions were addressed. The family elected for Sarah to grade skip. She would finish off the year in Grade 5 and her class teacher would work with Sarah to identify any gaps.

Sarah was unsure how to inform her peers. She waited a while before confiding in some close friends and it was announced later to the whole class. She was concerned about being asked lots of questions by her peers and she was provided with some phrases she could use to deflect or halt the questioning.

Sarah's decision came with considerable consequences. Socially, she would be missing a Year 6 graduation, and the celebrations and special events that students often look forward to as the leaders in the school. Financially, there were considerations for her scholarship. Her scholarship was due to end at the end of Year 6, and scholarship exams had already occurred earlier in the year for the Year 7 cohort she would be part of. The school carried her existing scholarship over into Year 7, and she sat the scholarship exam the following year.

The transition for Sarah was well-planned, ensuring meetings with teachers prior to the new school year commencing. The family knew they could contact the Gifted Education teacher with any concerns, and there were regular, informal, check-ins scheduled for Sarah. It wasn't all smooth sailing at the start as Sarah experienced uncomfortable questioning whilst on a camp at the start of the year.

Years later, Sarah and her family now reflect on this intervention. Even through skipping a year level, she still felt unchallenged in her learning, and feels that the benefit of skipping didn't pay off – other than being able to finish school a year earlier. All of the planning and discussions didn't counteract or accommodate Sarah's social anxiety. This was masked at the time, and for many years later, by her desire to please the adults in her life.

Sarah's experience is not reflective of all learners who skip a grade. It does however highlight the need to fully explore whether this intervention is appropriate in the first place, and how necessary it is to check in with the learner and their teachers.

An example of a transition plan is shown in Appendix B at the end of this chapter.

Year 7 in an Australian school and an example of a template that can be used to explore appropriate options can be found in Appendix B.

Grade skipping usually involves skipping one year level ahead; however in some cases, radical grade skipping may be more appropriate. Radical grade skipping is when the student skips at least two years ahead of the chronologically based grade level. An example of this is from a K-12 school in New South Wales that placed a Year 6 student with a Year 10 Extension Maths class[12]. This student was already two years younger than the rest of her Year 6 class, and her mathematical abilities were well-advanced. After testing, the school determined the Year 10 class to be a good fit, even though there were gaps in the learner's knowledge, and established a trial period. After six weeks, the move became permanent.

We cannot assume that a singular jump in year-level-based content will be sufficient to meet the learning needs of high-ability students. Even after a grade-skip, acceleration and additional interventions will need to be used. Gaps can be addressed and shouldn't be a reason to hold a student back. Be bold (radical) in thinking about how you can meet learners' needs. Is it reasonable to expect a Year 6 primary teacher to be able to meet the mathematical learning needs of this student? If so, what resources are available to use with this student? For K-12 schools, access to specialist teachers is less of an issue, particularly if campuses are in proximity. For standalone primary schools, is there a former student studying the domain at university that could be an appropriate tutor to offer some small group classes? Can you pool resources with other schools in the area faced with the same issue?

Early access to university units

For students in senior secondary (Years 11 and 12), many Australian universities offer an extension program allowing students to complete first year units that can accrue credits to be used towards a future course. Each university has its own application process and entry requirements along with a list of available study areas. There are online and on-campus options.

Withdrawal programs

Withdrawal or pull-out programs occur when a group of students are withdrawn from their usual class to work with another teacher/specialist on extension or enrichment activities or specific program (e.g., Maths focus). These programs may run on a weekly basis and the duration will vary, depending on the nature of the program. For example, if the group is working on an entry for a competition, they meet for four weeks in the lead up to the competition and perhaps a week post competition to evaluate and reflect on their process/product. Other programs may last a term, a semester, or be a year-long commitment. There are several decisions that need to be made when establishing a withdrawal program:

1. What types of programs will be developed?
2. What is the purpose of each program? Who is it targeting and why?
3. How will students be selected for participating in these programs? How will this be communicated with parents/carers?
4. When will the classes be scheduled? Will it be during class time? How will this impact other classes, especially specialist classes in a primary setting? Can a rotating timetable be established? What happens with missed classwork or when tests are scheduled?
5. How will the learning that occurs during these programs be reported to families and other teachers in the school? An example of a letter sent to families at the commencement of a withdrawal program is provided in Appendix C.
6. How will the programs be reviewed and evaluated?

> I loved being in [withdrawal] programs...not only was I challenged, but I was able to work with people who understood me...sometimes I felt slightly intimidated but it was somewhere I could make mistakes and not be judged.
>
> – Ella (Year 11)

Working through these questions will ensure the programs are set up for success from the beginning. There needs to be clearly communicated and defensible guidelines that steer the implementation of any withdrawal program.

It's all in the planning: ways of modifying our lessons

In addition to the interventions listed above, there are modifications that can be made to the learning environment, content, processes, and products to better meet the wide-ranging learning needs of students[13]. For high-potential learners, it is important to consider how the learning and behavioural characteristics of this group will influence the ways teachers can modify these elements of teaching and learning. Table 3.3 provides an overview of these characteristics and the ways in which each element of classroom teaching and learning can be modified accordingly. These characteristics are general in nature and will not apply to all high-ability learners.

There may be questions from colleagues or parents when implementing these modifications and interventions about fairness and limiting opportunities for other learners. Why should this student or group of students be able to do X and the others have to do Y? On the surface, the modified learning may look like fun. There are three questions you can use to determine whether the modification is specific to the high-ability learner(s) or the whole group, known as Passow's Test of Appropriate Curriculum[14]:

1. Would all students want to be involved in such learning experiences?
2. Could all students participate in such learning experiences?
3. Should all students be expected to succeed in such learning experiences?

> I most enjoy learning when I'm able to investigate things that interest and frustrate me, especially when I don't have to worry about a grade or a project
>
> – Rowan (Year 10)

If the answer is 'yes' to these questions, then the opportunity should be afforded to all students as there is insufficient differentiation to be applicable only to high-ability learners.

In sum, the basic modifications for high-ability learners in any classroom should be[15]:

1. Accelerate the pace of teaching and learning, particularly when mastering the basics
2. Engage students through problem-based learning and research, including problem solving and problem finding (design thinking process, inquiry is useful for this)
3. Focus on issues, themes, and ideas to encourage interdisciplinary connections.

Table 3.3 Modifications and learning characteristics

Element for modification	Learning/behavioural characteristics	Modifications
Learning environment: includes the role of learner/teacher, degree of independence, openness, acceptance, complexity, groupings, flexibility, and high mobility	• Independent, self-directed • High levels of curiosity • Flexibility • Enthusiastic • Highly focused on areas of passion • Perseverance (in areas that matter to them)	• Increased levels of independence • Encourage student initiative • Be open to changes in discussions or directions • Be open to students' ideas and interests • Flexible and adaptable teaching (content and strategies) • Access to materials/resources to arouse curiosity and provide intellectual stimulation (puzzles, books, models, artefacts) • Use different groupings of students • Allow for flexible movement of students
Content: concepts, ideas, and information are appropriate, developmentally and organizationally	• Readily able to work with abstract ideas or concepts • Diverse interests and abilities • Intuitive • Strong critical thinkers • Voracious reader • Enjoy problem-solving and applying concepts • Creative, inventive • Constantly questions • Independence	• Abstractness: extending learning content to include higher levels of knowledge, e.g., working with generalizations and theories • Complexity: exploring the interrelated relationships within an area of learning • Variety: in learning domains (breadth and depth), as well as types of problems requiring divergent and convergent thinking • Organization: use interdisciplinary learning as it reflects real-life connections between ideas and concepts, may use themes to organize content • Study of people: focus on creative/gifted people, their personal, career, and social characteristics • Methods: learning and inquiry methods used by those within the domain (e.g., scientific inquiry, historical inquiry)

(*Continued*)

Table 3.3 (Continued)

Element for modification	Learning/behavioural characteristics	Modifications
Process: includes teaching methods and the ways in which students will think and learn about the content	• Faster rate of learning • Less repetition (drill and practice) required when learning new material • High expectations of self and others, can lead to frustration • Persistent • Goal-directed	• Inductive learning strategies including guided inquiry, problem-based learning, project-based learning, case-based learning, discovery learning, and just-in-time teaching • Use of higher order thinking skills. Helpful taxonomies include Blooms (cognitive), Williams (creative), SOLO (learning complexity) • Open-ended questions, activities • Freedom of choice – include topics, methods used, product, and the learning environment • Pace and rate of instruction can be sped up • Variety – use a range of learning processes • Group or team-based activities (like and mixed ability)
Product: the output of the learning (e.g., oral presentation, prototype, website), often used for assessment purposes	• Sense of justice • Interest in problem solving • Sensitivity, empathy for others • Moral commitment to work • High levels of moral judgement and idealism	Ideal products will: • address real problems or concerns • with an authentic purpose • be directed to an authentic audience • transform knowledge and understandings, rather than summarize • involve others in evaluation, rather than just the teacher • be selected by the student

Adapted from Clark, B. (2002). *Growing up gifted: Developing the potential of children at home and at school* (6th ed.). Merrill/Prentice Hall and Maker, C. J., & Schiever, S. W. (2010). *Curriculum development and teaching strategies for gifted learners.* Pro-ed.

Underachievement

Gifted underachievement is often used to describe learners who are achieving or performing at levels lower than expected based on their high potential. There can be some contention around this topic with questions about definitions, obligation to perform at an expected level, who determines the level of 'potential', and does this create a ceiling of sorts?

A more practical way to consider underachievement is when you have

- students in your class that have a history of high achievement that declines (rapidly or over time)
- students that are performing at lower levels than reports from previous would predict
- students who may contribute to discussions, are clearly knowledgeable and display several high-ability characteristics (good and bad), but don't complete any work, or work is poorly (but rapidly) done.

There are many reasons why students may be underachieving, and they don't relate to laziness. In fact, up to 50% of high-ability students will underachieve at some stage throughout their education[16]. Underachievement is something that is learned, not an innate personality trait. Remember the talent development theories highlight the need for resources (inter- and intra-personal included) and support. It may be that lack of resources are inhibiting the student from achieving at a level commensurate with their abilities. This may be connected to family environment, or it may be the lack of opportunity and recognition at school, where too much drill and repetition and slow pace of learning has led to disengagement.

Table 3.4 indicates the various factors that may lead to underachievement in students.

Many of the strategies to support students who are underachieving involve the curriculum modifications listed in Table 3.3, for example, providing intellectually challenging content, provide authentic learning experiences (replicates real world), providing choice of topic, process, and product. In addition, students can be supported by[17]:

- setting learning goals
- providing timely, effective feedback
- establishing time management, planning, and organization strategies (including how to break tasks in manageable chunks)

Table 3.4 Factors leading to underachievement

Factor	Description
Low self-esteem	Leads to feelings of not being able to meet expectations of high performance
Attribution of success, fixed mindsets	Success is attributed to luck or task difficulty rather than effort or ability
Avoidance behaviours	Learning activities may be deemed irrelevant, or risky in exposing areas of relative weakness (e.g., if I don't study and don't do well, then it's because of no preparation rather than trying and not being able to do it)
Perfectionism	Procrastination, all-or-nothing type behaviours
School climate	Competitive, rigid, teacher-centred classrooms contribute to underachievement
Family climate	Competition between siblings, disruptions, or traumatic events (e.g., divorce, death)
Peer pressure	Pressure to conform to the peer group and 'dumb down' to not be the 'smart one' and different to the others
Lack of challenging/ rewarding educational experiences	Provision is unchallenging and irrelevant to learning needs, student disengages due to feeling unseen or neglected by learning design
Gender	Social gender norms and traditional work-family beliefs contribute to messages of male and female learners (e.g., boys are better at STEM, girls are better readers, writers)
Mental or physical health	May be short- or long- term illness impacting ability and/or motivation to engage in learning
Twice-exceptional	Focus on disability rather than providing opportunities to demonstrate or develop high-ability areas

Adapted from Davis, G. A., Rimm, S. B., & Siegle, D. (2011). *Education of the gifted and talented* (6th ed.). Pearson.

- providing study techniques to assist with focus (e.g., Pomodoro)
- listen and learn from the student about what they think is impacting their learning.

Taking it further

Innovative pedagogies

Each year, The Open University publishes a report on innovative pedagogies that appear to be promising, but yet to be implemented widely[18]. These reports provide an overview of various new pedagogical approaches, along with the potential impact and the anticipated timescale for widespread adoption. The first report was published in 2012 and featured assessment for learning and inquiry learning!

This resource provides teachers with exposure to new ways of working with all students. However, as the focus in this book is about high-ability students, there is no shortage of pedagogies that would be particularly relevant to this group and allow for differentiation within the class. Two pedagogies featured in these reports will be explored in more depth using case studies: design thinking (2016 report) and student co-created teaching and learning (2021 report).

Design thinking

Design thinking is increasingly being used in schools and provides opportunities for students to work at their own level, and can be set up in a way that allows students to tap into their interests and passions. Design thinking draws on the processes designers use when creating or developing new products or solutions. There are various models that can be used, with Stanford d.school (https://dschool.stanford.edu/) offering a simple, effective step-by-step process that is well-supported with resources for teachers and students. The British Design Council provides another approach with their double-diamond model and has resources available on their website (https://www.designcouncil.org.uk/).

In essence, there are five steps to the design thinking process:

1. Empathize: learn about your intended user
2. Define: state, clearly, what the problem is based on your user's needs
3. Ideate: generate ideas
4. Prototype: develop/build a model of the solution
5. Test: try out the prototype and refine as necessary

Through this process, students develop skills in eight core abilities[19], all of which are well-suited to the characteristics of and curriculum modifications for high-ability learners (refer to Table 3.3):

1. Navigating ambiguity
2. Learning from others (people and contexts)
3. Synthesizing information
4. Experimenting rapidly
5. Moving between concrete and abstract
6. Building and crafting intentionally

7. Communicating deliberately
8. Designing your design work

The following example of a design thinking unit was developed for a Year 9 mainstream cohort that included a range of abilities.

The task: Students were tasked with defining and developing a solution for a local issue that was connected to one of the UN's Sustainable Development Goals (SDGs).

The assessment: Student teams pitched their solution to a panel of 'experts', drawn from industry and academia. The panel nominated the solutions they believed had the most relevance and potential for impact. Students developed a portfolio demonstrating the skills they were developing throughout the process.

Duration: One term (approx. 10 weeks)

Organization:

Students were able to form their own groups, with a recommended size of 4–6 team members.

This was an addition to the structured timetable. Three full-day forums were planned (off campus) throughout the term that provided opportunities for guest speakers and exploration of and interaction with the local environment. In addition, students had a 45-minute block each week to work together, and time was also provided through English and Geography classes.

1. Forum One: Designed as a provocation, with speakers discussing homelessness and the impact of colonization on local first nations peoples.
2. Forum Two: Exploration of and interaction with local context to define problem and begin thinking of solutions.
3. Forum Three: Teams finalized presentations and pitched their ideas.

The process:

Empathizing: Students were introduced to the SDGs and spent time exploring the areas in which they were most interested. As a team, they explored the local context, physically as well as digitally, to explore the ways the selected SDG manifests. They spent time talking to people beyond the school and observing environments. The 'classroom' became the local environment.

Defining: Using the information they had gathered through observations, online research and interviews, teams defined their problem, and this guided their ideation.

Ideation: Teams spent time brainstorming a range of different solutions. They explored what solutions might already exist and researched what was feasible to implement.

Prototype and test: Once teams decided on their solution, they developed a working prototype they could test out on others and refined as necessary prior to the presentation to the panel.

The outcome:

This project demonstrated the power of students having agency in their learning. Whilst there can be some discomfort in shifting the focus to developing common skills and competencies, rather than common content knowledge, the observable growth, motivation, and commitment in students soon allay those concerns. There were teams that developed amazing ideas, such as setting up a market place for second-hand equipment and clothing that is required for a Year 9 camp experience. They recognized that much of the clothing, etc. is only worn whilst away, and that the cost (financial and environmental) can be reduced by on-selling these items second-hand. A Health and well-being program designed by teenagers for teenagers is another example, picking up on specific age-related issues and concerns and developing an app that could educate, support, and connect young people with resources and organizations. By removing many constraints, including the four walls of the classroom, students were able to find purpose and authenticity in ways that challenged them.

Student co-created teaching and learning

Pedagogical co-design involves teachers and students working together to design or amend new teaching and learning experiences, including assessments[20]. Student agency in learning and having choice in what they learn and how they learn it has been a feature in this chapter. Involving students in the design of learning experiences can seem challenging, with questions about knowledge, experience, and understanding of how people learn.

The design thinking example described above was developed in conjunction with students. A diverse group of students were invited to be part of a working party where they provided their input at the beginning stages of the unit design (structure, process, current frustrations, etc.) and then throughout the development phases. Given the open-ended nature of the project, input mainly centred on timing, locations, structure, and assessment.

Another example of co-created teaching and learning was a group of high-ability students leading the work in developing twenty-first century competency-based assessment rubrics that would be used across the entire school[21]. This involved them undertaking a great deal of research to establish what each competency entailed and what it might look like. After developing a draft framework, they worked with teachers and industry partners for further refinement. This was a big project that has real and ongoing effects in the school. The students involved had the capacity and motivation to fully engage and consider the complexities of the competencies.

There are limitations in this approach in that student involvement may be restricted to those who are willing and able to take part in the design. However, insights and contributions from those who are at the receiving end of learning design are valuable and opportunities to build this in are particularly beneficial for high-ability learners.

Summary

Providing high-ability learners with appropriate educational opportunities requires intentional planning and modifications to the learning environment, content, processes, and products. Identifying what students already know and what they are ready to learn next will help ensure these learners experience one year's growth for each year of schooling. There are a range of interventions that may be drawn on to provide the appropriate learning activities, including various forms of acceleration, withdrawal programs, and curriculum compacting. In addition, the characteristics of high-potential students inform the ways in which the four elements of learning design can be modified to better suit their learning needs.

Chapter Reflection

1. In what ways do you currently cater for the learning needs of high-ability students in your school/classroom?
2. Identify three small changes you will make to your learning design that will complement the characteristics of high-ability learners?
3. Identify three long-term goals targeting ways for improving provision, curriculum, and pedagogies as a whole school.

Notes

1 Griffin, P. (2018). Assessment as the search for evidence of learning. In P. Griffin (Ed.), *Assessment for teaching* (2nd ed., pp. 14–25). Cambridge University Press.

2 https://www.australiancurriculum.edu.au/f-10-curriculum/structure/

3 Victorian Curriculum and Assessment Authority. (2015). *Victorian Curriculum F-10: Revised curriculum planning and reporting guidelines.* https://www.vcaa.vic.edu.au/Documents/viccurric/RevisedF-10CurriculumPlanningReportingGuidelines.pdf

4 Department of Education and Training. (2018). *Through growth to achievement: The report of the review to achieve educational excellence in Australian schools.* Commonwealth of Australia.

5 Goss, P., Sonnemann, J., & Emslie, O. (2018). *Measuring student progress: A state-by-state report card.* https://grattan.edu.au/wp-content/uploads/2018/10/910-Mapping-Student-Progress.pdf

6 Wiliam, D. (2017). *Embedded formative assessment: (Strategies for classroom assessment that drives student engagement and learning).* Solution Tree.

7 Rogers, K. B. (2015). The academic, socialization, and psychological effects of acceleration: Research synthesis. In S. G. Assouline, N. Colangelo, J. VanTassel-Baska, & A. Lupkowski-Shoplik (Eds.), *A nation empowered: Evidence trumps the excuses holding back America's brightest students* (pp. 19–29). The Connie Belin & Jacqueline N. Blank International Center for Gifted Education and Talent Development Centre.

8 Rogers, K. B. (2007). Lessons learned about educating the Gifted and Talented: A synthesis of the research on educational practice. *Gifted Child Quarterly, 51*(4), 382–396.

9 Southern, W. T., & Jones, E. D. (2015). Types of acceleration: Dimensions and issues. In S. G. Assouline, N. Colangelo, J. VanTassel-Baska, & A. Lupkowski-Shoplik (Eds.), *A nation empowered: Evidence trumps the excuses holding back America's brightest students* (Vol. 2, pp. 9–18). Benin-Blank Centre, College of Education, University of Iowa.

10 Reis, S. M., Renzulli, S. J., & Renzulli, J. S. (2021). Enrichment and Gifted Education Pedagogy to Develop Talents, Gifts, and Creative Productivity. *Education Sciences, 11*(10), 615. https://www.mdpi.com/2227-7102/11/10/615

11 Winebrenner, S. (2001). Teaching gifted kids in the regular classroom. *Minneapolis, MN: Free Spirit.*

12 Chalwell, K., & Cumming, T. M. (2019). Radical subject acceleration for gifted students: One school's response [Other Journal Article]. *Australasian Journal of Gifted Education, 28*(2), 29–46. https://doi.org/10.21505/ajge.2019.0014

13 Maker, C. J., & Schiever, S. W. (2010). *Curriculum development and teaching strategies for gifted learners.* Pro-ed.

14 As cited in MacLeod, B. (2005). *Gifted and talented professional development package for teachers: Module 5.* Gifted Education Research, Resource and Information Centre, The University of New South Wales.

15 VanTassel-Baska, J., Feldhusen, J., Seeley, K., Wheatley, G., Silverman, L. K., & Foster, W. (1988). *Comprehensive curriculum for gifted learners.* Allyn & Bacon.

16 Siegle, D. (2018). Understanding underachievement. In *Handbook of giftedness in children* (pp. 285–297). Springer.

17 Ibid.

18 The Open University. (2022). *Innovating Pedagogy*. Retrieved 25 January from https://www.open.ac.uk/blogs/innovating/?p=774

19 Hasso Plattner Institute of Design at Stanford University. (2023). *About*. Retrieved 25 January 2023 from https://dschool.stanford.edu/about

20 Kukulska-Hulme, A., Bossu, C., Charitonos, K., Coughlan, T., Ferguson, R., FitzGerald, E., Gaved, M., Guitert, M., Herodotou, C., & Maina, M. (2022). *Innovating pedagogy 2022: exploring new forms of teaching, learning and assessment, to guide educators and policy makers* (147303678X). The Open University.

21 Barnes, M., Lafferty, K., & Li, B. (2022). Assessing twenty-first century competencies: can students lead and facilitate the co-construction process? *Educational Review*, 1–19.

APPENDIX B: ACCELERATION PLAN

This is a document that maps out acceleration options and provides families and teachers with a clear understanding of options and implications.

Student Name:

DOB:

Current year level:

Current teacher:

Assessment data:

Test	Norms	Stanine	Percentile

Scholarship data (if applicable):

Provide description of student background, experience, and interests.

Rogers (2015) identifies forms of subject-based acceleration and grade-based acceleration. Grade-based acceleration allows students to progress more quickly through school, thus leaving the school system earlier.

Subject-based acceleration provides a more focused intervention allowing students to extend their knowledge, skills, and understandings beyond their current year level. All forms of acceleration have varying effect sizes, i.e., the degree of impact on the learner.

Accelerated classes	Description	Effect size
Compacted curriculum	Time saved from eliminating/ reduced content is used for more advanced content or enrichment	Academic: slight Social: moderate Psychological: slight
Online courses		Academic: strong Social: Psychological: moderate
Concurrent enrolment:	Attends Yr 7 classes when in Yr 6	Academic: moderate
Grade skipping	Learners bypass one or two years	Academic: strong Social: moderate Psychological: moderate
Independent study	Students are provided a structure for in-depth study of a topic of interest during the school day	
Individualized acceleration	Students work at their own pace through continuous progress content and skill areas	Academic: slight Social: Moderate Psychological: Moderate
Mentorship/ coaching	Placement with a content expert to extend learning in the content area	Academic: slight Social: strong Psychological: slight
Single-subject acceleration	Students bypass the usual progress in ONE subject, progressing normally in others	Academic: moderate Psychological: moderate
Telescoping curriculum	Instruction is provided that entails less time than is normal, e.g., One year in 6 months. Always results in advanced grade placement	

When considering options, we need to be aware of the dimensions of acceleration and related concerns, as outlined in the table below (Rogers, 2010).

Dimension	Concerns
Pacing	Calibration, reporting, continuity of the process over the years
Salience	Age of student, stage of schooling, type of acceleration
Peers	Knowledge of the acceleration by others, type of acceleration, group or individual, degree of acceleration
Access	Population centres, acceptability by school, state policy, cost, availability of courses or program, transportation
Timing	Age-related issues, during school vs outside of traditional school time

Pathway 1: Grade skipping	STUDENT X will finish her time in Year 4 and will begin Year 6 in the next school year, thereby skipping Yr 5 *Telescoping of curriculum* would occur in the last 6 months of Yr 4 in preparation for progression into Yr 6	**Advantages:** **Considerations:** **Peers:** **Pacing:** **Access:** **Salience:** **Timing:**
Pathway 2: Single-subject acceleration	Withdraw STUDENT X from her Yr 4 class to work with Yr 6 Maths class	**Advantages:** Student X would be extended in her area of talent **Considerations** **Salience:** **Peers:** **Pacing:** **Access:** **Timing:**
Pathway 3: Curriculum Compacting	Based on evidence, STUDENT X's teachers would eliminate drill and practice of known content, essentially bypassing those areas that are already known. The time saved can be directed towards providing enrichment opportunities for STUDENT X, such as 1. Extended projects/investigations developing her understandings and skills in a variety of interest areas 2. Extended competitions 3. Teaching her advanced concepts in the same sub-strand on which the rest of the class is focusing	**Advantages:** **Considerations** **Salience:** **Pacing:** **Access:** **Timing:** **Peers:**
Pathway 4: Online course, independent study	Online course/independent study	
Pathway 5: Mentoring/ coaching		

Short Term vs Long Term

The main criteria when deciding on an appropriate course of action to best develop STUDENT X's expertise are **effectiveness** and **sustainability**.

Recommendations:

School Based: Given the information in the table, identify what the school feels is the best way forward

External: Identify external resources or actions the family can access outside of school to support the learner

APPENDIX C: LETTER TO FAMILIES REGARDING WITHDRAWAL PROGRAM

Dear Families

This term, _____, will be participating in the **Digital Storytelling** group as part of the Enrichment Education program. This group will continue throughout Term 2.

Digital storytelling provides students to explore and introduce elements of storytelling that is not possible with traditional hard copy texts as they use computer-based tools and software to enhance their story. We will be using Photostory 3 to create our digital stories.

As a group, we will examine the elements that contribute to effective digital storytelling such as music, narration, video, and images. Students will then apply these understandings and skills to create one of the following projects:

a. retell a myth of choice putting a modern twist on it
b. create a biography on a person of choice
c. an original narrative written by the student.

If you have any questions, please contact me via email at [insert email address here]

4 Diversity

BACK TO BASICS

Within education, teachers are aware of the diverse needs of a mixed-ability classroom: diverse learners with diverse learning needs. This chapter focuses on the ways in which diversity can hinder the talent development of gifted students. In particular, gender and sexuality diversity, cultural diversity, and students with additional learning needs (twice exceptional) are introduced. The implications for talent development are discussed along with ways in which these can be mitigated with practical strategies and examples.

Schools have always been diverse settings, with classrooms full of individuals with unique needs. The mainstream classroom groups all students together and the role of the teacher is to ensure this mix of learners is an inclusive and positive environment for all. This means meeting the learning and social emotional needs of all learners and removing any barriers to their learning and growth[1]. It also means providing experiences and opportunities to recognize, acknowledge, and learn about the identities of all learners. This chapter builds on from the previous chapter to provide a more nuanced discussion about ways in which to work with diverse high-ability students.

It's tempting to think about high-ability students as one group of students with similar needs. And while there are generalizations that can made about the types of educational experiences that are more suited for this group (see Chapter 3), gifted students are more different than they are alike.

Diversity comes in many forms including cultural, socioeconomic, neurological, religious, linguistic, gender or sexual, and academic. Learners will

DOI: 10.4324/9781003267973-4

have multiple identities based on the intersections of the multiple aspects of their background and life. The following sections will explore some of these diverse identities within the context of high-ability learners.

Twice-exceptional learners

Twice-exceptional students (briefly discussed in Chapter 2) are those who have both high ability in at least one domain, as well as a disability. The disability may be physical or sensory (e.g., hearing impairment), developmental (e.g., ADHD or ASD), learning (e.g., dyslexia), or psychosocial (e.g., anxiety). The focus for this group of learners is often the disability, rather than the high levels of talent, leading to a deficit rather than a strength-based approach. A study of 13,000 children with an identified disability reported that only 11% of 300 who scored in the 90th percentile on a norm-referenced achievement test were participating in gifted and talented programs[2] (refer to Chapter 2 for more on identifying twice-exceptional learners).

Working from a strengths-based, talent development perspective means there needs to be a focus on how to support the learner to develop their talents and to ameliorate potential barriers that disabilities may present. This means speaking with the learner, their family, and allied health professionals, all of whom will have expert knowledge about effective strategies and appropriate adjustments for that learner.

Personalized learning is identified as a way of ensuring that all learners are successful and builds on their strengths[3]. There are three guiding principles when working to personalize learning for all learners:

1. Quality teaching and learning: providing effective and purposeful learning experiences to build on talents, making appropriate adjustments where required
2. Consultation: providing opportunities for everyone involved to contribute to the discussion about the adjustments that will be made (i.e., student, family/carer, allied health or other relevant people, school staff)
3. Collaborative practice and planning: ensuring that this is a shared goal, with everyone, including the principal, making sure that needs are met, and communicating planning in an appropriate time and manner.

Step 1: Know your student	Step 2: Consult	Step 3: Plan and implement	Step 4: Evaluate the impact
• What is their background, what are their strengths, interests, goals? • What types of adjustments might be appropriate or required?	• Speak with the student, family/carer • Seek expert advice about the needs of the learner • Continue consultation with student and family/carer	• Identify interventions, adjustments, supports • Design learning tasks, materials, etc. • Identify and source any equipment, assistive technology, etc. • Select appropriate teaching strategies • Plan monitoring and review process	• Evaluate the success of the measures with student, family/carer, other teaching staff. • What else might need to be implemented? What's next?

Figure 4.1 Steps to planning personalized learning

There are four steps to guide the process when planning personalized learning[3], shown in Figure 4.1. Knowing the student is an obvious starting point. It is vital to not only recognize strength but to know what the learner is ready to learn next in their talent domain.

> From a social perspective, the challenges that able kids who are also neuro-diverse is significant and not well addressed in school, particularly primary school. Even when high performing kids are neuro-typical, the difference in cognitive development can sometimes mean that forming friendships with age peers can be challenging as well, and that is also not well supported. There tends to be a 'well, they are just different' or 'they like to be alone' view taken at primary school, in particular, rather than a recognition that this is a problem of timing and age, everyone needs a tribe, and so this needs to be actively managed to avoid long term self-esteem issues for the child.
>
> – Teresa (parent)

To achieve this, we need to have the skills and knowledge to provide the educational experiences and environments that facilitate the talent development of twice-exceptional students. Whilst the research in the area of specific interventions for high-ability students' talent and disability domains is sparse, there are three disability domains that are most frequently researched: Autism spectrum disorder (ASD); attention-deficit/hyperactivity disorder (ADHD); and specific learning disorder (SLD)[4].

Autism spectrum disorder (ASD)

ASD affects social, behavioural, and communication functioning[5]. As a developmental condition, people with autism will have different needs and challenges, and *up to 20% will have exceptional or above average skills in areas including maths, art, reading, mechanics, memory, and music*[6]. Table 4.1 provides an overview of some of the characteristics of ASD. It is estimated that approximately 353,880 Australians are on the autism spectrum, with four times as many boys as girls. And whilst the number of males diagnosed may be higher at this time, Autism Spectrum Australia suggest that there are more females with autism than currently diagnosed[7]. Theories for this discrepancy include

1. Current diagnosis process is biased towards traditional male norms
2. A focus on other health concerns and possible (mis)diagnosis of anxiety, depression, or eating disorders
3. Missed diagnosis due to traditional female gender norms (e.g., quiet, shy) and a greater motivation to interact with peers
4. Mimicking social behaviours to camouflage challenges.

It is important for teachers, both those with a Gifted Education specialist role and mainstream, to understand the strengths and characteristics of high-ability students with ASD to ensure that the strengths of this twice-exceptional group are recognized and developed in appropriate ways. A recent Australian study found that the parents (29%) were more likely to report an 'exceptional skill' than teachers (17%)[8]. This makes sense in that parents and teachers are likely to observe different behaviours in the different settings. Assumptions about student behaviour and capacities can be limiting and deny students with ASD the opportunity to flourish and develop their areas of talent. Drawing on the characteristics and advice from allied health professionals, national and state associations, we can work with the student themselves and their family to develop a range of interventions, adjustments, and supports that are appropriate for that individual.

It is not within a teacher's purview to diagnose students, but if we have concerns based on behavioural observations indicating developmental challenges or delays, then we should certainly raise these concerns with families. Indeed, children with milder challenges may not be recognized until they are in the school environment[9]. This needs to be approached with sensitivity and

Table 4.1 Characteristics of autism

Domain	Characteristics
Strengths and interests	Persistent, eye for detail, retention of facts and figures, deep interests in typical or non-typical topics Ability to maintain strong focus on areas of interest
Social interactions	Uncomfortable in busy or complex social interactions Does not require eye contact to pay attention Social interactions often misunderstood by others May prefer to work/play independently or alongside others
Communication	Honest and direct Difficulty with or dislike of small talk, sarcasm, understanding jokes Repeating words/phrases that seem out of context Not using or understanding gestures
Leisure and play	Prefers to spend time on passions Engages in non-traditional play Preference for doing things the same way Comfortable with using technology to socialize (e.g., online chats, games)
Sensory	May feel overwhelmed or distressed if there is sensory overload (e.g., bright lights, sounds) Draws on strategies to avoid overwhelm such as blocking out sounds Seeking sensory experiences, and greater awareness of some sensations (e.g., smells, tastes, touch)
Thinking	Ability to concentrate for a long time on one thing Notices specifics that others do not (e.g., details, changes, patterns) Changing from one thing to another is difficult
Emotions – experience and expression	May experience a strong, emotional connection with others Delayed understanding and regulation of emotions May use repetitive movements when responding to emotions (e.g., stress or excitement) Difficulty in understanding how non-autistic people think and respond in situations
Adapted from Autism Spectrum Australia. (n.d.). *About autism.* https://www.autismspectrum. org.au/about-autism	

different families will respond in different ways. Teachers can provide support and guidance with assessments or organizing a meeting with the school's student services team. A case study (see Box 4.1) describes an experience of working with a student from first meeting to discuss observed developmental challenges through to putting a personalized learning plan in place.

Box 4.1 Case study: Autism spectrum disorder

A Year 7 student, Anand, begins at a new high school. His teachers notice how he enjoys speaking with them one on one and will often stay after the lesson has concluded to have these conversations. Sometimes he sends a teacher an email with an image or story he enjoyed. There is a hyperfocus on topics of interest.

Anand has a very mature sense of humour which can be quite dark at times. He enjoys sharing one-liners and jokes with his teachers. It is clear to his teachers that he is a bright student. He enjoys working on his computer and playing games. He uses the chat function to engage with other players and will speak up and defend others on the chat if he sees something he feels is wrong. He has a number of interests, including making things out of art and craft materials and he is clearly very creative.

Anand's teachers become frustrated with him during their lessons as he doesn't complete the set work and can be distracted in class. Homework is incomplete and he often doesn't have the materials he needs for the lesson. Some of the learning activities are collaborative, and Anand is expected to work with a small group of his classmates. He wanders around the room during this time, and the teachers suspect he is trying to avoid doing any extra work. The teachers know Anand is a creative and insightful thinker, and that he has advanced skills in several domains. They lament that they can't seem to get him to produce any work.

Due to some behavioural concerns, Anand's pastoral teacher and coordinator began consulting with the family to learn more about his primary school years. There had been some challenges with teachers and peers, but no follow-up actions had been taken.

The school recommended that Anand's family arrange for a cognitive and behavioural assessment. Rather than focus only on a potential behavioural diagnosis, it was important that his cognitive abilities be affirmed. This was not just for those working with Anand to understand what he was capable of, but also, and more importantly, for Anand to understand this too. Due to his interactions and experiences at school up to this point, Anand felt that all teachers hated him, that he was a problem, and that no one really wanted to be around him. Anand had a very negative self-image and felt that all his actions were intentional on his part.

Results of the testing indicated that Anand had ASD and his cognitive ability was in the superior range. This provided a frame for Anand, his family, and his teachers to understand the reasons behind some of his behaviours and pointed to interventions that would be appropriate for Anand to build on and develop his strengths.

Follow-up conversations with Anand and his family shed light on some small ways teachers could change their lessons to provide opportunities for success and growth. Some of the immediate practical strategies included:

- providing harder work but less questions
- present work in chunks so the number of questions is spread across different pages and is less overwhelming than seeing a full page of tasks to be done
- encourage using Pomodoro (timed periods of focus) to try and resist the 'urges to do something' (as Anand described)
- use discrete tasks, providing achievable start and end points of the activity
- short activities with a definite and clear goal, providing opportunities to feel like he has been successful in completing the task
- for bigger tasks, break them down into clear steps that are discrete and relatively short in duration
- making sure the steps and expectations of the lesson were recorded on the learning management system or apps that were used by the class for teaching and learning, e.g., Google classroom or MS Teams
- the conditions around assessments needed to be adjusted. For example, additional time for planning a written response.

Some useful site for ASD resources and information include:

https://allplaylearn.org.au
https://www.autismspectrum.org.au
https://www.amaze.org.au/

Attention-deficit hyperactivity disorder (ADHD)

Attention-Deficit Hyperactivity Disorder is a neuro-developmental disorder that results in difficulty controlling impulsive, inattentive, and hyperactive behaviour affecting one in 25 Australians, including approximately 298,000 children[10]. It is estimated that there is an additional 75% of those with ADHD that are undiagnosed, with girls often being under-identified with less disruptive hyperactive behaviour (i.e., fidgeting, talkative, emotional reactivity)[11]. Unfortunately, adolescents with ADHD are approximately ten times more likely to experience depression than teens without ADHD[12].

In terms of school experiences, a survey of parents and carers[13] revealed that 36% of parents of children with ADHD reported an absence of any adjustments to learning provisions (teaching, activities, assessments). Behaviour management strategies, punitive and exclusionary, were overused and that one on three students changed schools due to issues connected to ADHD.

ADHD has many positive characteristics associated with the ways in which behaviours manifest[14]. For example, those with ADHD are often:

- curious
- imaginative
- creative
- innovative
- hyper focused on areas of interests
- enthusiastic
- spontaneous
- adventurous

These characteristics are not dissimilar to those of high-ability students in Table 3.3 that were linked to teaching and learning modifications. In fact, the overlapping symptoms of high ability and ADHD mean it is vital to work with students and families to determine the best way to support the learner[15]. Focusing on strengths and supporting students in areas like executive functioning tasks and well-being will help. In addition, adjustments to assessments, learning activities, and teaching strategies will ensure opportunities are provided for a child with ADHD to thrive.

Some useful site for ADHD resources and information include:

https://www.adhdaustralia.org.au/
https://adhdfoundation.org.au/adhd
https://www.adhdsupportaustralia.com.au/

Specific learning disorder (SLD)

Specific learning disorders (SLD) is a term that is used to describe neuro-developmental disorders that impact learning academic skills (i.e., writing, reading, mathematics) such as dyslexia (reading), dyscalculia (mathematics), and dysgraphia (writing)[16]. In Australia, it is estimated that up to 10% of the population have a learning disorder, with the most common being dyslexia (approximately eight in ten of those with a SLD)[17].

As with ASD and ADHD, a student with a SLD can also have high ability, although they may not have had the appropriate support to demonstrate this, or the focus may be on the disorder rather than on the areas of strength. Given the prevalence of SLD with an impairment in reading (i.e., dyslexia) and the written nature of many assessments, using identification and selection tools that are timed or use global (total) scores may obscure a learner's strength in a sub-test. Allowing and providing supportive technologies such as voice-to-text and vice versa can relieve the cognitive load and allow students to demonstrate what they can do, without being held back by the SLD. Allowing more time for learners to complete assessment or reducing the amount of written text in assessments will also provide greater opportunity for them to reveal what they can achieve.

Of course, any additional provision (e.g., enrichment) should also be supported appropriately and discussed in collaboration with the learner and their parents or carers. Respecting and utilizing the learner's position in knowing their own learning preferences and tools that work for them will lead to greater success of any interventions. There are several state and national organizations that are a great source of information, strategies, and training for teachers and schools to assist students with a SLD.

Some useful site for SLD resources and information include:

https://auspeld.org.au/
https://dyslexiaassociation.org.au/
https://dsf.net.au/

Cultural and linguistic diversity

Australia is a multicultural society. In 2021, 27.6% of the population were born overseas[18] and in addition to having the oldest continuous cultures, there are more than 270 ancestries that Australians identify with[19]. Linguistically, almost a quarter of Australians speak a language other than English at home and 48.4% of the Australian-born people who did speak another language at home were children under 15 years of age[20]. Whilst the degree of cultural and linguistic diversity will vary from one area to another, and one school to another, diversity exists demanding we consider the needs of culturally and linguistically diverse (CLD) gifted learners.

Cultural and linguistically diverse students can be underrepresented in Gifted Education programs, although this seems to be dependent on the socio-educational advantage (SEA) of the CLD families. The latest reports from MySchool website[21] indicate the enrolments at high-ability, select entry schools have a majority of language background other than English (LBOTE) students ranging from 86% to 90%, with only 4% of students representing the bottom quarter for SEA. Over half the student population of all four select entry schools in Victoria are from the top quarter for SEA (ranging from 59% in an outer suburban school to 86% in an inner-city school). This enrolment pattern is also found in Sydney's select entry schools, with socioeconomic advantage featuring amongst its enrolments[22].

Underrepresentation of CLD students in gifted/high-potential programs is a national (and international) issue, with variation in the degree of opportunities some cultural groups are offered compared to others[23]. In Australia, indigenous educational disadvantage is a focus in the 'Closing the Gap' framework with education-specific targets including provision and opportunity for students to reach their full learning potential and to receive a tertiary education (see https://www.closingthegap.gov.au/partnership for more information). Underrepresentation can occur for several reasons, all of which are identified in the talent development theories presented in Chapter 1 and include:

- undervaluing of talents/gifts, leading to lack of identification and recognition
- lack of, or insufficient, external resources and support
- mismatch of how 'success' is defined, e.g., focus on scholastic achievement rather than on leadership or creativity or other strengths
- cultural biases in assessment used for selection purposes.

If we consider that many programs rely on academic achievement tests to select students for specially designed programs, then we need to also consider that these tests may not be fair for all students. For example, in the regional area of Dubbo, NSW, a group of researchers randomly administered either the standard version of NAPLAN or a version that had been modified to be more culturally appropriate through local contextualization by the NSW Aboriginal Education Consultative Group[24]. Whilst this study found no effect on student scores in Numeracy, there were meaningful effects for the Reading outcomes. In fact, for Indigenous students, the use of the contextualized test would increase their NAPLAN scores by 25 points, which places them in Band 5 and closes the achievement gap for indigenous students by 50%. Whilst this was a small study, it does show that a test score can be a result of the test itself, and not necessarily reflective of student ability.

When narrow 'selection' or identification tools and strategies are combined with a Western view of what high ability or giftedness 'looks' like, barriers and blind spots to identifying and serving indigenous students are exacerbated. The Differentiating Model of Giftedness and Talent reminds us there are many forms of gifts, falling under several domains and can therefore be represented and understood in many ways.

Different cultural groups will view giftedness or high ability in different ways. One indigenous view of giftedness is that it includes 'your knowledge of your ancestry, your land, your kin, and your respect for your community and elders.' (p. 3)[25]. Others have described indigenous giftedness through linguistic, spatial, interpersonal, and naturalist and spiritual intelligences[26]. As with all groups, it is important to recognize that there is not a one-size-fits-all approach, particularly in the case of indigenous Australians where there are over 250 mobs (tribes) with their own language and dialects[27], and each family will have their own histories and knowledge.

What are three things mainstream, non-indigenous teachers should know about working with indigenous students?

1. Our cultural backgrounds, values and knowledge are extremely varied but doesn't mean that students are more or less Indigenous than someone else.
2. Our family, peoples and ancestors experience doesn't mean that students should be expected to teach the class, rather recognize that the student may experience trauma. If a student offers a personal

perspective, teachers should value this and rather than see this as opportunity to 'probe' for more, reflect that you have likely created a culturally safe space for the student to speak up. Use this as an opportunity to find out how to continue this and potentially share with other teachers.

3. Understand the importance of Country and place. Part of the difficulty for Indigenous people can be their ability to connect to place. By undervaluing or not encouraging this connection, students could become disengaged before they begin. I think this is where it becomes important for schools to connect with their local Indigenous communities (not just Traditional Owners) to assist in staff understanding this concept

– Michael (Barkindji and Wemba Wemba man)

When working with CLD students, it is important to recognize and value those gifts and use alternative strategies for identification. A successful example of this is dynamic testing using the Ravens Standard Progressive Matrices (RSPM), a non-verbal instrument measuring general intelligence, and a metacognitive intervention between pre- and post-testing[28]. The metacognitive intervention mimics the items on the RSPM and students are guided through their thinking and ways of approaching the items. The results from this indicated that dynamic testing was an effective approach to identifying high potential.

Often Indigenous people are taught to work within a community but there is often a hierarchical structure that doesn't translate well into the school environment. I could learn with my cousins, ask questions of my parents, aunts and uncles but I knew that when Nan spoke, you listened and moved. It is difficult for schools to create an environment where questions can be asked without perceptions or impressions being confined to the classroom.

– Michael (Barkindji and Wemba Wemba man)

Students from diverse cultural and language backgrounds are not preprogrammed to be one type of learner or another. Cultural identities can shape motivation and learning through a match or mismatch of the learning context and the cultural expectations. Rather, the behaviours for and attitudes towards learning are developed and reinforced at both home and school. Understanding and recognizing cultural norms and histories that shape classroom interactions with adults and peers will go a long way to building trusting relationships with students and communities and protect and celebrate cultural identities.

Sexuality and gender diversity

There isn't a lot of research on this population of gifted students, but when we draw from wider research figures, it becomes clear that we need to become much more deliberate and intentional in our schools to address their diverse needs.

A recent survey of 6,418 LGBTQA+ young people (aged 14–21 years) from across Australia provides an eye-opening snapshot of what is happening in our schools[29]. For example,

- 27.3% of secondary school respondents reported there was an absence of supportive or inclusive discussion of LGBTIQA+ people
- 60% had felt unsafe or uncomfortable at some stage in the previous 12 months because of their gender or sexuality diversity
- 38.4% of secondary school respondents indicated they were absent from school in the previous 12 months due to feeling unsafe or uncomfortable
- 63.7% reported they frequently heard negative comments about sexuality at their school
- 28.1% indicated they had experienced verbal harassment in the previous 12 months, with schools being the most likely environment for this to occur (compared to university and TAFE settings).

The mental health and well-being among this group are concerning. High or very high psychological distress amongst 16- to 17-year-old participants was more than three times higher than the general population in the same age group (83.3% compared to 27.3%).

For gifted LGBTIQA+ students, there may be an added sense of difference and isolation, referred to as 'twice different', stemming from feeling different because of high ability as well as feeling different due to identity[30]. The intersectionality of giftedness and identity amplifies the challenges for high-ability students.

It was very difficult for me to understand how my sexuality and gifted-ness interacted in my school environment. The sense of being 'other' was already entwined into my sense of identity, and I didn't have the skills to follow the threads. At primary school I'd found it easier to hang out with the girls, but I knew I didn't belong there, so I did my own thing. At the time I only understood my giftedness to mean 'good at school work', and so couldn't see that the sensitivity that can come with being gifted was heightened by the sensitivity which comes from being a gay man. The same was true for my creativity.

– Dan (gifted adult)

It is important for gifted LGBTIQA+ students, as with all individuals, to see themselves reflected within day-to-day teaching and learning activities. Without positive validation of identity, there is a risk that students will disconnect from their learning. Some of the barriers students have identified include[31]:

- homophobia, transphobia
- lack of teacher training when working with LGBTQIA+ students
- power dynamics
- responsibility for educating others falling on the student

Ways that highly able LGBTIQA+ students can be supported include[32,33]:

- Listening to and understanding their needs
- Providing ways for them to make difference (real-world problems and issues)
- Developing a true understanding of diversity, this includes identity
- Encourage different perspectives, include issues relating to LGBTQ+
- Consider examples/scenarios/materials used in class activities. Use positive diverse examples of LGBTQ+ people who have made valuable contributions to science, maths, arts, etc.
- Being cognisant of our own implicitly held biases and stereotypes – are assumptions forming the basis of pathway/interest recommendations
- Being cognisant of the language we use ensuring it is inclusive, non-gendered. Small acts such as using your pronouns on your email are valued
- Offering support in face of challenges, many are willing to self-advocate to improve conditions for themselves and others, but there are also instances

where students will disclose to teachers and not parents for any number of reasons. This needs to be respected

- Developing school policies
- Establish/join school-based gay/queer, straight alliances, e.g., Rainbow Club
- Keep learning about ways to support LGBTQ+ people.

Summary

Australia is a diverse country, with diverse communities, diverse schools, and diverse classrooms. When working with high-ability or high-potential students, it is essential we look beyond the dominant cultural view of gift-edness and consider how individual students may demonstrate their ability in idiosyncratic ways. High-potential students learning English may not be able to express themselves as articulately as others, but this doesn't mean they should be excluded from programs or opportunities that meet their other learning needs, likewise for students with ADHD, ASD, or a SLD. Students need to have their identities recognized and valued through positive representations and engagement in learning activities. When high-potential students do not receive appropriate educational experiences, they can develop feelings of frustration, disengagement and question their abilities. Getting to know the student, their identities, families, communities, histories, perspectives, and the ways of drawing out valuable cultural funds of knowledge will go a long way in meeting the needs of diverse high-ability learners and avoid preventable negative consequences.

Chapter Reflection

1. How diverse is your school? In what ways is this diversity represented in
    a. Specialized programs, clubs?
    b. High-potential programs (specifically)
    c. Learning and teaching practices
2. What strategies do you use to identify high-potential students who may be 2e or CLD?

3. Are there any groups that are unrepresented in Gifted Education provisions in your school?
4. Identify some actions you can take to ensure equitable access to extension/enrichment opportunities (e.g., financial or geographical barriers)?

Notes

1 Finkelstein, S., Sharma, U., & Furlonger, B. (2021). The inclusive practices of classroom teachers: a scoping review and thematic analysis. *International Journal of Inclusive Education*, 25(6), 735–762. https://doi.org/10.1080/13603116. 2019.1572232, Heathdirect. (2021). *Learning disabilities.* https://www.health direct.gov.au/learning-disabilities#:~:text=In%20Australia%2C%20up%20to%20 1,a%20learning%20disability%20have%20dyslexia

2 Barnard-Brak, L., Johnsen, S. K., Pond Hannig, A., & Wei, T. (2015). The incidence of potentially gifted students within a special education population. *Roeper Review*, 37(2), 74–83.

3 Education Services Australia. (2020). *Planning for personalised learning and support: A national resource.* Education Services Australia. https://www.nccd.edu. au/sites/default/files/planning_for_personalised_learning_and_support.pdf

4 Foley-Nicpon, M., & Kim, J. Y. C. (2018). Identifying and providing evidence-based services for twice-exceptional students. In *Handbook of giftedness in children* (pp. 349–362). Springer.

5 Foley-Nicpon, M., & Assouline, S. G. (2020). High ability students with coexisting disabilities: Implications for school psychological practice. *Psychology in the Schools,* 57(10), 1615–1626. https://doi.org/10.1002/pits.22342

6 Autism Spectrum Australia. (n.d.). *About autism.* Retrieved 14 December, 2022 from https://www.autismspectrum.org.au/about-autism

7 Austism Spectrum Australia. (n.d.). *Girls and women on the autism spectrum.* https://www.autismspectrum.org.au/uploads/documents/Fact%20Sheets/ Aspect-Research-girls-and-women-on-the-autism-spectrum.pdf

8 Clark, T., Jung, J., Haas, K., Gibbs, V., Roberts, J., Robinson, A., & Howlin, P. (2020). *Perceptions of exceptional skills in children with autism.* https://www. autismspectrum.org.au/uploads/documents/Research/Exceptional-skills-of-children-report.pdf

9 AllPlay. (2022). *Information about diagnosis.* Monash University. https:// allplaylearn.org.au/primary/teacher/information-about-diagnosis/

10 ADHD Australia. (2019). *What is ADHD?* https://www.adhdaustralia.org.au/ about-adhd/

11 ADHD Australia. (2020). *13 Myths about ADHD.* https://www.adhdaustralia. org.au/wp-content/uploads/2020/10/ADHD-Myths-Factsheet-1-Final.pdf

12 Ibid.

13 Parents for ADHD Advocacy Australia. (2019). *Parent and carer experiences of ADHD in Australian schools: Critical gaps*. Parents for ADHD Advocacy Australia. https://parentsforadhdadvocacy.com.au/wp-content/uploads/2020/09/ADHD-Final-Survey-Interactive-PDF.pdf

14 ADHD Australia. (2019). *What is ADHD?* https://www.adhdaustralia.org.au/about-adhd/

15 Foley-Nicpon, M., & Kim, J. Y. C. (2018). Identifying and providing evidence-based services for twice-exceptional students. In *Handbook of giftedness in children* (pp. 349–362). Springer.

16 Moll, K., Kunze, S., Neuhoff, N., Bruder, J., & Schulte-Körne, G. (2014). Specific learning disorder: Prevalence and gender differences. *PLoS One, 9*(7), e103537.

17 Heathdirect. (2021). *Learning disabilities*. https://www.healthdirect.gov.au/learning-disabilities#:~:text=In%20Australia%2C%20up%20to%201,a%20learning%20disability%20have%20dyslexia

18 Australian Bureau of Statistics. (2022). *Cultural diversity of Australia*. https://www.abs.gov.au/articles/cultural-diversity-australia#measuring-cultural-and-ethnic-diversity

19 Australian Human Rights Commission. (2014). *Face the facts: Cultural diversity*. Australian Human Rights Commission,. https://humanrights.gov.au/our-work/education/face-facts-cultural-diversity

20 Australian Bureau of Statistics. (2022). *Cultural diversity of Australia*. https://www.abs.gov.au/articles/cultural-diversity-australia#measuring-cultural-and-ethnic-diversity

21 Australian Curriculum Assessment and Reporting Authority. (2023). *My school*. Retrieved 24 January from https://www.myschool.edu.au/

22 Tham, M. (2021). *School selectivity and socioeconomic and academic stratification in metropolitan Sydney and Melbourne* (CIRES Working Paper 02/2021, Issue. Centre for International Research on Education Systems.

23 Chandler, P. (2011). Prodigy or problem child? Challenges with identifying Aboriginal giftedness. In W. Vialle (Ed.), *Giftedness from an Indigenous perspective* (pp. 1–9). AAEGT. https://ro.uow.edu.au/cgi/viewcontent.cgi?article=1016&context=uowbooks

24 Dobrescu, L., Holden, R., Motta, A., Piccoli, A., Roberts, P., & Walker, S. (2021). *Cultural Context in Standardized Tests*. https://papers.ssrn.com/sol3/papers.cfm?abstract_id=3983663

25 Chandler, P. (2011). Prodigy or problem child? Challenges with identifying Aboriginal giftedness. In W. Vialle (Ed.), *Giftedness from an Indigenous perspective* (pp. 1–9). AAEGT. https://ro.uow.edu.au/cgi/viewcontent.cgi?article=1016&context=uowbooks

26 Gibson, K., & Vialle, W. (2007). The Australian Aboriginal view of giftedness. In S. N. Phillipson & M. McCann (Eds.), *Conceptions of giftedness* (pp. 197–224). Lawrence Erlbaum Associates.

27 Deadly Story. (n.d.). *Aboriginal people.* https://deadlystory.com/page/culture/articles/World_s_Indigenous_Peoples_Day/Aboriginal_people

28 Chaffey, G. W., Bailey, S. B., & Vine, K. W. (2015). Identifying high academic potential in Australian Aboriginal children using dynamic testing. *Australasian Journal of Gifted Education; v.24 n.2 p.24–37; December 2015*, 24(2), 24–37. https://doi.org/10.21505/ajge.2015.0014

29 Hill, A.O., Lyons, A., Jones, J., McGowan, I., Carman, M., Parsons, M., Power, J., & Bourne, A. (2021) Writing Themselves In 4: The health and wellbeing of LGBTQA+ young people in Australia. National report, monograph series number 124. Australian Research Centre in Sex, Health and Society, La Trobe University.

30 Parra-Martinez, A., & Treat, A. R. (2022). The rainbow revolution: Empowering gifted LGBTQ+ learners for transformative action. In R. J. Sternberg, D. Ambrose, & S. Karami (Eds.), *The Palgrave Handbook of Transformational Giftedness for Education* (pp. 287–312). Springer International Publishing. https://doi.org/10.1007/978-3-030-91618-3_15

31 Ibid.

32 Ibid.

33 National Association for Gifted Children. (n.d.). *LGBTQ diversity toolbox for teachers - instructional strategies.* https://www.nagc.org/lgbtq-diversity-toolbox-teachers-instructional-strategies

Social Emotional Development and Well-Being

BACK TO BASICS

The link between well-being and learning is well established and there are some common areas to be aware of to help high-potential learners thrive. These characteristics are identified and described with tips and strategies to support these students. The asynchronous development that can occur within this group can be misunderstood and this is explained in more detail. The role of the psychosocial skills for gifted learners is highlighted in the ways that these can affect talent development. Concerns related to transitions, particularly from primary to secondary, are identified. The consequences of a mismatch between curriculum and learning needs are discussed and the mediating role that early identification and intervention can have.

TAKING IT FURTHER

Betts and Neihart provide profiles of the gifted and talented that highlight the needs, feelings, and behaviours of six different categories that high-ability learners may fall into. These are explored in detail.

What is social emotional well-being?

It is established that social emotional competence can be developed over time and it enables the management of emotions, establishment of meaningful and supportive relationships, development of healthy identities, achievement

DOI: 10.4324/9781003267973-5

of personal and collective goals, and the ability to make considered, responsible decisions[1]. These types of skills and competencies may also be referred to as psychosocial skills[2]. As with all competencies, this is not something to be left to develop by chance, or osmosis, rather the skills, knowledge, understandings, and attitudes of social emotional competence can be explicitly taught. This is evident in the inclusion of the Personal and Social general capability in the Australian Curriculum[3].

A useful framework for social emotional learning is the CASEL (Collaborative for Academic, Social, and Emotional Learning) framework, or CASEL wheel, that identifies five core competencies of social emotional development[4]:

1. Self-awareness
2. Self-management
3. Social awareness
4. Relationship skills
5. Responsible decision making.

Schools have different ways of teaching these sub-capabilities, with various forms of well-being programs regularly being implemented across classrooms for all ages and stages. They may be ready-made programs that have been purchased or a more bespoke, in-house offering. Regardless, they have, at least in my experience, often been delivered as a one-size-fits-all model, and in one school I used a program that even provided scripts for the teacher. This may be a successful approach for many schools, however, when it comes to high-potential students, there is a layer of complexity to their social emotional development that can be linked to asynchronous development.

Asynchronous development refers to the uneven social, intellectual, emotional, and physical development of high-ability learners. Imagine a 6-year-old student at school. Physically, she is the same size as everyone else, same motor skills, but she has the cognitive development of a 10-year-old. She is a voracious reader, devouring chapter books at home. Her imagination, vocabulary, and story-telling reflects this. In class, she either refuses to write or at other times relies on the support from her teacher to help her get started. When asked about why she finds it difficult to write, she explains that she can't get her ideas down quickly enough, and when she does, it doesn't look the way she wants it to look.

Asynchronous development can cause frustration for high-potential lean-ers through misguided expectations from not only themselves but others assuming that because they may be able to converse on topics like someone many years older, that they should have the same level of social skills and emotional regulation. Some of the behaviours or traits that may be linked to asynchronous development can be ameliorated through the deliberate and explicit development of social emotional competences. Table 5.1 provides definitions, examples for each of the CASEL competencies[5], along with con-cerns or issues related to high-ability learners.

There can be an assumption that high-ability students will be fine left to their own devices. They learn quickly, and often independently, don't strug-gle academically and therefore attention can be directed to other, more at risk students. This type of thinking is also reflected in the 'elitist' view of Gifted Education, i.e., that already privileged learners are being provided with addi-tional opportunities for even greater success. The remainder of this chapter will highlight some common areas that teachers can work with high-ability students to circumvent some of these issues for each competency.

Self-management

When teachers are asked to identify high-ability students in their classroom, they will often pick the students who are compliant, motivated, and eager to please. These students do their work without prompting and complete it to a high standard. However, not all high-ability students will present in this way. Consider a student who has never been sufficiently challenged in a learning environment: they coast through the work, leave it until the last minute to com-plete it, or never need to study for a test. They might be the ones who end up with comments like 'they distract others' on their reports. Or the student who has always been praised for how 'smart' they are and has an acute awareness of the high expectations set by themselves, their parents, their teachers, and even their classmates. One of the issues that may manifest for them is perfectionism.

Perfectionism

Perfectionism is not always a negative. In fact, perfectionism can be catego-rized broadly as normal or neurotic with the difference lying in the degree of mistakes that are tolerated and satisfaction with the quality of performance[7].

Table 5.1 CASEL competencies, definitions, and examples

Competency	Definition	Examples	Issues or concerns related to high ability/giftedness[6]
Self-management	Ability to manage emotions, thoughts, and behaviours effectively in different contexts and to achieve goals	• Setting goals (personal and collective) • Demonstrating agency • Using planning and organizational skills (e.g., time management) • Managing emotions • Manage stress • Self-motivation and self-discipline	• Undeveloped study skills • Frustration in day-to-day life (intellectual) • Anxiety, depression • Perfectionism • Insufficient challenge at school • Emotional intensity
Self-awareness	Ability to understand emotions, thoughts, and values and know how they affect behaviour	• Knowing own strengths and weaknesses • Sense of confidence and purpose • Having a growth mindset • Developing interests and sense of purpose • Self-efficacy • Integrating personal and social identities • Being honest and integrous	• Competitive or avoidance of competition • Failure-avoidance • Difficulty determining a philosophy of life • Difficulty with self-discovery and understanding • Big-fish-little-pond effect
Social Awareness	Ability to understand perspectives of and to empathize with others	• Understand social norms for behaviours in different contexts (e.g., classroom, playground) • Recognize diverse social norms (including those deemed unfair/unjust) • Have compassion and empathy for others • Recognize and value strengths in others • Expressing gratitude • Consider others' perspectives	• Difficulty in understanding cognitive differences • Nonconforming and challenge or resist authority • Difficulty working in groups

(Continued)

Table 5.1 (Continued)

Competency	Definition	Examples	Issues or concerns related to high ability/giftedness[6]
Relationship skills	Ability to establish and maintain healthy and supportive relationships	• Cultural competency • Develop positive relationships • Communication effectively • Conflict resolution • Demonstrating leadership • Practicing teamwork and collaborative problem-solving skills • Defend the rights of others • Seek and offer help when required	• Difficulty connecting with peers, leading to social isolation • Dumbing down or hiding talents to fit in with peers • Difficult teacher relationships
Responsible decision making	Ability to make caring and constructive choices about behaviour and interaction in diverse contexts	• Demonstrating curiosity and open-mindedness • Identifying solutions for personal/social problems • Make reasoned judgements using information, data, and facts • Anticipate and evaluate the consequences of actions	• Many interests make it difficult to focus on specific areas/makes choices (multipotentiality) • Insufficient challenge at school • Behavioural issues

Adapted from: Collaborative for Academic Social and Emotional Learning (CASEL). (2023b). *What is the CASEL framework?*

> The one thing that worries me most is that my child is her worst critic and this makes herself to be her own worst enemy. It is not lack of confidence but being harsh on herself. Always there is scope of improvement and thus after a certain point a person needs to move on but for my daughter she will think of improvement even though the task is submitted.
>
> – Monira (parent)

Normal perfectionism is flexible and whilst high standards are set, the degree of precision is adjusted depending on the nature of the task. Neurotic perfectionists, however, adopt a zero-tolerance approach, with any minor mistake or dissatisfaction rendering the performance pointless. Perfectionism can be further described in terms of five dimensions including[8]:

1. High personal standards
2. Perception of high parental standards
3. Perception of high parental criticism
4. Doubting the quality of one's actions
5. Preference for order and organization.

The dimensions may manifest in procrastination, inability to complete a task, unrealistic standards, highly critical, focus on results, driven by fear of failure and making mistakes, disproportionate response to lower-than-expected results or outcomes, defensive to constructive feedback, excessive time spent on making lists and organizing, and excessive checking of understanding or standard of task[9].

> A lot of gifted/smart kids end up with awful self-esteem issues because they tie their self-worth and their value as a person to their intelligence. I can speak to that personally. If you start telling a kid you expect more from them, they will feel crushed under the weight of that. Don't give us a bar to jump over, just make the ceiling higher so there's more room to jump if you can.
>
> – Rowan (Year 10 student)

The prevalence of unhealthy or problematic perfectionism is unclear. An American estimate suggests that 20% of high-ability students experience some level of neurotic perfectionism[10], while an Australian study reported no greater likelihood for these students than non-gifted participants to have unhealthy levels of perfectionism[11]. However, the overall scores tended to be higher and gifted students were more likely to be perfectionists than the non-gifted group. Areas in which the high-ability cohort scored higher were personal standards, concern over mistakes and parental expectations and criticism. These levels increased with year level.

Ways teachers can support students with perfectionism include[12, 13]:

- Emphasizing effort rather than the result
- Help develop positive self-talk
- Discuss difference between excellence and perfection
- Bibliotherapy (using stories to address affective needs)
- Provide safe opportunities to take academic risks
- Help develop timelines, break tasks down into manageable tasks, and recognition of when less precision is okay.

Box 5.1 Stories about perfectionism

- Beautiful Oops! By Barney Saltzberg
- Dot by Peter H Reynolds
- Ish by Peter H Reynolds
- Penelope Perfect by Shannon Anderson
- The good egg by Jory John and Pete Oswald
- The most magnificent thing by Ashley Spires
- The book of mistakes by Corinna Luyken
- The girl who never made mistakes by Mark Pett and Gary Rubinstein
- The crocodile in the bedroom by Arnold Lobel

Learning how to learn: motivation, commitment, persistence

Students who never, or rarely, have to navigate appropriate challenges in their learning run the risk of never learning how to learn. If academic learning comes easily, with little effort and no perseverance, how do you learn to learn? How do you learn to persist and apply effort if you have never had to do it? If these opportunities don't occur during the years of compulsory education, then the first exposure may occur at university. This isn't ideal given the structure and independent nature of tertiary education. The vignette in Box 5.2 demonstrates the importance of providing challenging learning experiences, and the opportunity to fail, to develop the motivational skills and emotional regulation skills required for learning.

Box 5.2 Vignette: Importance of learning how to learn

It is only recently that I have wondered what it would have been like to learn to learn. By this I mean the specific skills of learning, rather than merely learning content. For all of my primary and secondary education, the teaching I received was based on reaching a certain standard. With the exception of one or two topics (I'm thinking of integration and differentiation!), I was able to quickly grasp a concept once it had been presented, and so never really had to persist with the uncertainty, discomfort, and frustration of not being able to understand. Those few topics where I couldn't grasp the core concept, then I could usually get by with replicating the solution. The result was that I could strive to be the best student in the class, year, and school without needing to deal with the failure of not achieving it.

This strategy started to come unravelled at university, where there were people who were either smarter than me or prepared to sacrifice more to achieve the results they wanted. I felt very unprepared for this, and had a lot of difficulty with my mental health. The solution I came up with was to just abandon a subject which wasn't going well, even if the cut-off for unenrolling had passed. I believed it was better to fail a subject by not attending the exam, than to get an average result. In third year, I was called in to see the Assistant Dean, which was routine when someone has failed as many subjects as I had. Instead of my silent call for help being answered, however, he seemed to get distracted by how good my first-year results were, and how I would have been one of the top students of the year. I still didn't get any help with learning persistence and learning to risk failure.

The longer term effect of this seems to have been that I interpreted failure (and that includes everything below being exceptional) as a sign that I was pursuing the wrong path and that I needed to move to something different. It was only in my early 40s that I let myself take up painting as a hobby on the basis that I was to enjoy it at whatever level of skill I exhibited. As it was, my first painting at an introductory painting course turned out to be pretty good! Developing my skills as an artist was the first time that I've consciously been aware of working through the frustration of not being able to manifest what I wanted, and to persist in refining my capacity and openly accepting my limitations.

– Dan (gifted adult)

Emotional intensity, moral sensitivity

Emotional intensity is often referred to in relation to the social and emotional development of high-ability learners and describes the increased strength, frequency, and duration of emotional reactions amongst this group[14]. Indeed, heightened intensity leading to qualitatively different experiences and awareness forms the basis of one definition of giftedness[15]. Moral sensitivity and a strong sense of justice have also been associated with giftedness. This may result in learners becoming distressed or anxious about world events and issues such as climate change. Watching the news, or hearing about disasters, natural or manmade, may cause these learners to become more upset than their age peers. They may feel greater depths of compassion for those experiencing hardship or be particularly sensitive to the actions and reactions of others. They may ruminate for longer about the causes and consequences and may feel despondent about what can be done.

In many cases, this is explained through emotional overexcitability. Overexcitabilities are one part of a theory called Positive Disintegration that was developed by Polish psychologist and psychologist, Kazimierz Dabrowski. There is debate amongst some in the field of Gifted Education and those who are familiar with Dabrowski's work about the degree to which overexcitabilities are particularly relevant to the gifted. One of the biggest criticisms comes from the focus only on the 'overexcitabilities' without considering the remainder of the theory. There are also questions about the measurement properties of the instrument used in the overexcitability research with gifted populations. Others argue that this can be explained through being open to experiences, or a combination of both[16]. My advice if you are interested in learning about overexcitabilities is to access the freely available online resources and learn about them within the context of the entire theory.

Regardless of 'why' there seems to be a pattern of increased emotional intensity and moral sensitivity, understanding that some high-ability learners may have more heightened reactions can shape the support and strategies teachers can offer in the classroom.

Social awareness

Although some students may display the emotional and moral sensitivity described above, this is not to say it will be evident in all high-ability students or evident in the day-to-day interactions with peers. Anecdotally, I have heard many teachers express their frustrations about the attitudes and behaviours of high-ability students in their mainstream classrooms. I'm sure everyone has experienced being in a class, as a learner or teacher, and having another student comment, loudly, how *easy* a task is, or yell *'FINISHED'* at the top of their lungs to ensure the whole class is aware that they have finished first (and quickly). A perception of arrogance and lack of understanding of how this may make their classmates feel can be irritating to everyone in the class. Group work can be fertile ground for complaints with some proclaiming the high-ability student 'takes over' and is 'bossy' or the high-ability learner declaring that they have to do all the work, or it won't be good enough.

> I've had a builder working on my house, and a number of times I've had to decide whether to point out a better way of solving something. My life feels like a delicate balance of when to call out a truth (as I see it at least), and when to let it pass. Not everyone wants to know that the emperor isn't wearing any clothes, least of all the emperor!
>
> – Dan (gifted adult)

Of course, these examples are generalizations but I'm sure at some level are relatable and proof that social awareness needs to be taught. Ways of doing this include:

- Pointing out to students how their declarations of 'easy' and quick finishing may make other students feel is a good starting point.

- Encouraging them to see the strengths that other group members bring that they don't will also help them recognize and value their teammates.
- Introducing and using protocols for team/group work will promote constructive collaborative practices.

Relationship skills

Asynchronous development of high-ability learners may lead to feelings of social isolation and lack of age-based peers, but there is no conclusive research that suggests that this group is more prone to social issues or differ in their social development[17]. However, there are instances where some children have advanced levels of maturity and the nature of their interests, vocabulary, etc. may make it difficult for them to make meaningful friendships.

An Australian researcher, Miraca Gross, highlighted the need for 'true peers' and the 'forced-choice dilemma'[18]. The forced-choice dilemma describes the, at times, conflicting goals of seeking high levels of achievement and pursuing their interests and forming close friendships. The conflict arises due to the advanced cognitive, social, and/or emotional development. Consider the Year 2 child who shares her interest and vast knowledge of Mesopotamia with her classmates, who look at her blankly as they pick up discussion about fidget-spinners or whatever the latest toy 'fad' may be. Or the Year 7 child who is greatly concerned with social or environmental issues and embarks on an awareness campaign sharing her concerns with her peers and teachers. Or the child beginning school, who is already a capable reader as her peers spend time learning letters and sounds.

> In our case, our daughter picked concepts up within 5 minutes and then pretended for the rest of the class that she was working through it so that she wasn't singled out. So, provide the extra work at the start of the class and check up afterwards perhaps
>
> – Jodie (parent)

One of the effects of the forced-choice dilemma is that high-ability learners may go 'underground' and hide or camouflage their abilities[19]. They may stay quiet during class discussions or pretend they don't know the answers. They may do well at school, but not well enough to be different. They may change the language they use when with peers compared to when at home. True peers, or intellectual peers, provide high-potential learners with the opportunity to be themselves and share in their interests. This doesn't have to be at the expense of age peers. Rather, high-ability learners may have multiple friendships, with each meeting different needs and interests[20].

> I loved extension programs. They were my favourite parts of the week and the things I looked forward to most about school. They gave me the opportunity to connect with other people who shared my interests and outlook (many of whom I'm still friends with).
>
> – Rowan (Year 10)

Working with like minds is recognized as one the key considerations when working with high-ability learners[21]. Providing opportunities for high-potential students to work with like minds is one way of ensuring these learners can find true peers, and form friendships based on shared interests and commonalities rather than age. It also provides them with opportunities to engage with the learning activity at higher levels and evenly share the workload. These opportunities can be created through cluster groupings in classes, providing regular withdrawal programs (may be multi-age) or through special interest groups/clubs. Some settings provide permanent groupings such as high-potential classes or select entry schools.

> I do not think cognitive age is as important as ways of thinking about the world, or the ability to comprehend and respect other ways of being in the world. I think true peers emerge through relational contexts, and my personal experience of finding my peers entailed leaving all of my school friends behind, leaving home, and finding myself.
>
> – Greg (gifted adult)

Self-awareness

It seems reasonable to assume that students who achieve highly and learn quickly will be confident learners. They will be aware of and know their high abilities and this will be reflected in their level of self-awareness. Knowing oneself as a learner and having confidence and efficacy may not always be stable, rather this knowledge can be influenced by the setting and the social comparisons that are made within that setting. For high-ability learners, changes in settings that result in changes in social comparisons can result in dips in confidence and academic self-concept.

This is known as the big-fish-little-pond effect (BFLPE).

Transitions: big fish, little pond

The big-fish-little-pond effect (BFLPE) occurs when high-ability students transition from an environment where they were the 'smartest in the school' and used to being the best or at least one of a small group of the best into environments where there are many others just like them, if not better. This could be the student from a primary school of 400 students starting high school, where there are 200 students in their year level alone. It might be students commencing at a select entry school, or a first year Engineering student from a large but regional high school who finds themselves surrounded by students just like them. These students are used to comparing themselves to students of 'average' ability, and as such their academic self-concept is influenced by these social comparisons. With the change of context, the social comparisons begin to have a negative effect on their academic self-concept, even though their academic performance may not have changed.

The BFLPE occurs at all ages and is particularly pertinent for high school students when social comparisons, self-consciousness, and academic pressure are at their highest levels, but effects can be seen in primary and tertiary students as well[22]. This effect is consistent across cultures and geographic locations, so it seems that no one is immune. However, there are some indications that verbal academic self-concept is more susceptible than STEM or general academic self-concept.

Research has shown that there are moderating factors that can be drawn on to minimize the negative impact of the BFLPE. These include

- having a positive relationship with teachers (i.e., feeling at ease, understood)[23]
- focusing on individual learning rather than that of the whole class[24].

When working with high-potential students who are beginning in a new educational setting, whether that be a high-potential full-time class grouping, withdrawal group, select entry school, or for primary students transitioning to high school, an awareness of the BFLPE will help teachers support these students through these transitions.

Responsible decision making

The ability to make caring and constructive choices, considering the consequences of these choices, seems straightforward. All children need to learn, as best they can, to manage impulses, and to consider not just the consequences for themselves, but also for others. This type of social emotional learning begins in infancy. So how is this an area of potential concern for high-ability students? One of the answers comes in the concept of multipotentiality. Multipotentiality refers to having high abilities and interests in several domains leading to difficulty in making choices, particularly as it relates to making career-related decisions (e.g., choosing a tertiary course).

Multipotentiality

The literature around multipotentiality often refers to career-related decisions. The prevalence and impact of multipotentiality amongst high-ability students is contested within current literature with the impact of multiple interests and abilities being viewed as a positive leading to many opportunities[25]. However, there may be instances where it can negatively impact a high-ability student, not just in pathways and careers, but in in other ways too.

The vignette in Box 5.3 illustrates how well-intentioned praise led to self-questioning about the career choices Dan has made throughout his life and a realization that, for him, pathways determined by abilities alone were not the best way to make decisions. Similar versions of this can happen in schools, not just in the senior years of secondary schooling and career counselling, but through seemingly benign and well-intentioned opportunities and invitations.

When students are offered many opportunities, they may feel an internal or external pressure to do everything they can. Withdrawal programs for Mathematics, a lunchtime debate club, joining a sports team with after school training, playing an instrument, as well as additional competitions or one-off events that come along, all come with a commitment of time and effort. This is in addition to any activities or duties that need to be done

> **Box 5.3 Multipotentiality**
>
> One of the expressions that I have become wary of is 'You'd be good at that…'. For a long time whenever I heard this, I would re-evaluate my career, and think that this person had brought a new insight into where my career success and happiness might lay. Now I recognize that I have many skills, and that shaping my pathway based on them does not lead me to a happier place. It also means that my skills don't point to an obvious pathway. Instead, I am provided with a wide range of options, and my challenge has been to blend them in a way which feels authentic to me.
>
> – Dan (gifted adult)

outside of school. When students are fortunate enough to have many opportunities, there needs to be communication with the learner and their family about their commitments and strategies to manage their time. This includes learning how to say no and prioritizing.

Putting it altogether: practical tips and strategies

The preceding sections provide understandings and insights into the social emotional worlds of high-potential learners. As with all learners, the ways in which we can best support them will be variable depending on what is happening for them.

In the first instance, the most effective strategy is to develop and nurture a supportive relationship. Being open, non-judgemental, listening, and demonstrating care for the student fosters trust and the conditions to be able to better support them.

In my roles in schools, I have been asked to work with specific high-ability students who are having a difficult time. Usually, my brief was to help them with time management, organization, and/or study skills. Whilst this was what appeared to be the issue, on the surface at least, it was never that easy.

During a period of (pandemic-related) remote learning, I was asked to meet with a student for exactly the reasons above. She was behind in several subjects and the idea was that I could work with her to develop some strategies. It became apparent, quickly, that study skills were not the issue. Given the reliance on video calls, I had a difficult time getting our first chat happening even with amazing parent support. Our first chat was just that, a chat, talking about haircuts, baking and sharing recipes, and getting reacquainted after not having worked together for a few years. I explained why I wanted to speak with her and what I hoped we could achieve. She shared her views as well and we scheduled our next online catch-up. The success rate of sticking to our scheduled chats was about 50%, even with attempts from home to get her online. When we did chat, I wanted to remove the teacher-student hierarchy. I wasn't worried about language or swearing, she just needed to be able to speak freely. As school returned to face-to-face teaching, she had a hard time getting there. We planned to meet at the gate, but she just couldn't get there. She was already working with a psychologist on these issues and was very self-aware.

As she was entering senior secondary, discussions shifted to ways to support her throughout her final two years where expectations and workload increased. One option was completing her senior secondary certificate over three years. In one enlightening discussion, she commented that she could get onboard the transport to get to school, but just couldn't get off. It seemed clear that perhaps the school was no longer the right fit for her. She ended up taking the second half of the year off and enrolled in a new school the following year. It proved to be the perfect choice for her that allowed her to thrive. There was no way that study skills were going to help this.

Ways of helping and supporting students include:

- Ensuring they have a trusted teacher or school counsellor/psychologist they can go to when needed
- Making sure student needs are communicated to all relevant teachers. This may be through additional learning information on a student management system, or more informally through conversations. As with all well-being issues, details are not always appropriate nor necessary
- Using resources and additional supports, such as counselling or psychological services
- Communicating with parents. There may already be some established strategies used at home that can be adopted at school

- Talk with students about what it means to be gifted. A colleague developed a unit that focused on social emotional well-being that was used with primary school students where different topics, like perfectionism, were discussed. This provided an opportunity for students to share their experiences with one another and realize they were not alone in feeling this way or suffering from the debilitating effects. A level of self-awareness maximizes the effect of this type of program
- Using bibliotherapy. A great resource for this is a book called, 'Some of my best friends are books' by Judith Halsted. It provides a selection of books that are organized according to age groups and issues/themes
- Considering the underlying causes and if there are strategies that can be used and reinforced across all or many learning contexts (e.g., reinforcing growth mindset, self-talk)
- Providing opportunities for students to socialize (and play) with like minds through clubs and play (e.g., Lego Club, Coding Club, Magic the Gathering Clubs) where they can feel a sense of belonging and practice socialization and 'play' in a controlled environment with rules, social conventions, supervision, and goals
- Provide opportunities to establish their own groups based on their interests
- Involvement in school projects providing a purpose and interaction with others
- Adopt a strength-based approach, focusing on the positive psychological characteristics that build resilience (e.g., practicing gratitude to focus on positive aspects of life)
- Harnessing the unique, special qualities (passions, special interests) that may appear to be detrimental to the learning environment and seek productive and positive opportunities for these skills to be applied, e.g., using an 'IT hacker' to work with the IT department on special project
- Using behaviour support plans[26] developed in conjunction with the student, parents, and staff that identify the behaviours of concern (e.g., not completing work), triggers (e.g., perceived difficulty of the task), the function of the behaviour (e.g., failure avoidance), behaviour goal (e.g., complete tasks), proactive (prevent-teach-reinforce) interventions (e.g., self-talk) and evaluate the degree of success
- Explore, as a school, social emotional learning programs that are designed to improve emotional literacy, self-regulation, social relationships and build feelings of belonging and connectedness.

Taking it further

It has been mentioned several times throughout the preceding chapters that there is no one-size-fits-all and that high-ability learners in many ways differ more than they are alike. Betts and Neihart[27, 28] developed six profiles of gifted, talented, and creative learners that is useful for considering the different behaviours and needs of high-ability learners:

1. The successful
2. The creative
3. The underground
4. The at-risk
5. Twice/multi-exceptional
6. Autonomous learner

These are presented in Table 5.2 with details regarding their feelings/ attitudes, behaviours, needs, and the types of supports that can be offered by schools. Again, whilst based on generalizations, the profiles offer insights and may prompt teachers to take a closer look at the underlying causes of student behaviour. In this model, the aim for all students is to become autonomous learners, with all other profiles considered underachieving.

Summary

When asked about the skills and attitudes they hoped their high-ability children would develop by the time they concluded their secondary education, these parents responded with the following:

- *'independent thinking, analytical skills, being adaptive and open to change, an interest in lifelong learning, not being afraid to take on new challenges outside her comfort zone, the attitude of having a go, the ability to set attainable goals, the ability to embrace her mistakes and move on'* – Sally
- *'social skills and develop more confidence in terms of being comfortable with her achievements and not downplaying them'* – Jodie
- *'Rowan already knows the value of working hard to achieve outcomes, but I also hope that they know that life is about more than just hard work, and that they have the skills to nurture the non-academic skills essential to life as an adult, as well as the academic parts'* – Teresa

Table 5.2 Profiles of gifted, talented, and creative learners and associated needs/supports

Type	Feelings/Attitudes	Behaviours/Characteristics	Needs (at school and at home)	School Supports
The Successful	Complacent Dependent Good academic self-concept Fear of failure Extrinsic motivation Self-critical Works for the grade Unsure about the future Eager for approval Fixed view of intelligence	Achieves Seeks teacher approval Avoids risks Doesn't go beyond the syllabus Accepts & conforms Chooses safe activities Gets good grades Becomes a consumer of knowledge	To be challenged To see deficiencies To take risks Assertiveness skills Creativity development Incremental view of intelligence Self-knowledge Independent learning skills	Subject & grade acceleration Needs more than AP, IB, & Honours Time for personal curriculum Activities that push out of comfort zone Development of independent learning skills In-Depth Studies Mentorships Cognitive Coaching Time with Intellectual Peers
The Creative	Highly creative Bored & frustrated Fluctuating self-esteem Impatient & defensive Heightened sensitivity Uncertain about social roles More psychologically vulnerable Strong motivation to follow inner convictions Wants to right wrongs High tolerance for ambiguity High Energy	Expresses impulses Challenges teacher Questions rules, policies Is honest and direct Emotionally labile May have poor self-control Creative expression Perseveres in areas of interest (passions) Stands up for convictions May be in conflict with peers	To be connected with others To learn tact, flexibility, self awareness, and self-control Support for creativity Contractual systems Less pressure to conform Interpersonal skills to affirm others Strategies to cope with potential psychological vulnerabilities	Tolerance Reward new thinking Placement with appropriate teachers Direct & clear communication Give permission for feelings Domain-specific training Allow nonconformity Mentorships Direct instruction in interpersonal skills Coach for deliberate practice

(*Continued*)

Table 5.2 (Continued)

Type	Feelings/Attitudes	Behaviours/Characteristics	Needs (at school and at home)	School Supports
The Underground	Desire to belong socially Feel Unsure & Pressured Conflicted, Guilty, & Insecure Unsure of their right to their emotions Diminished sense of self Ambivalent about achievement Internalise & personalise societal ambiguities & conflicts View some achievement behaviours as betrayal of their social group	Devalue, discount, or deny talent Drops out of GT & advanced classes Rejects challenges Moves from one peer group to the next Not connected to the teacher or the class Unsure of direction	Freedom to make choices Conflicts to be made explicit Learn to code switch Gifted peer group network Support for abilities Role models who cross cultures Self-understanding & acceptance An audience to listen to what they have to say (to be heard)	Frame the concepts as societal phenomena Welcoming learning environments Provide role models Help develop support groups Open discussions about class, racism, sexism Cultural brokering Direct instruction of social skills Teach the hidden curriculum Provide college planning Discuss costs of success
The At-Risk	Resentful & Angry Depressed Reckless & Manipulative Poor self-concept Defensive Unrealistic expectations Unaccepted Resistive to authority Not motivated for teacher driven rewards A subgroup is antisocial	Creates crises and causes disruptions Thrill seeking Will work for the relationship Intermittent attendance Pursues outside interests Low academic achievement May be self-isolating Often creative Criticises self & others Produces inconsistent work	Safety and structure An 'alternative' environment An individualised program Confrontation and accountability Alternatives Professional Counselling Direction and short-term goals	Don't lower expectations Diagnostic testing Non-traditional study skills In-depth Studies & Mentorships Academic coaching Home visits Promote resilience Discuss secondary options Aggressive advocacy

(Continued)

Table 5.2 (Continued)

Type	Feelings/Attitudes	Behaviours/Characteristics	Needs (at school and at home)	School Supports
The Twice-Multi Exceptional	Learned helplessness Intense frustration & anger Feelings of inferiority Unaware Work to hang on Poor academic self-concept Don't view themselves as successful Lack of self-confidence Don't know where to belong	Makes connections easily Demonstrates inconsistent work Seems average or below More similar to younger students in some aspects of social/emotional functioning May be disruptive or off-task Are good problem solvers Behaviour problems Thinks conceptually Enjoys novelty & complexity Is disorganised Slow in information processing May not be able to cope with gifted peer group	Emphasis on strengths Coping strategies Skill development Monitoring for additional disorders – especially ADHD To learn to persevere Environment that develops strengths To learn to self-advocate	Challenge in area of strength is first priority Acceleration in area of strengths Accommodations for disability Ask, "what will it take for this child to succeed here?" Direct instruction in self-regulation strategies Give time to be with GT peers Teach self-advocacy Teach SMART goal setting
The Autonomous Learner	Self-confident Self-accepting Enthusiastic Accepted by others Supported Possess desire to know & learn Willing to fail Intrinsic motivation Accepts others Seeks personal satisfaction	Has appropriate social skills Works independently Develops own short-term & long-term goals Does not seek external approval Follows strong areas of passion Thinks creatively & critically Stands up for convictions Is resilient Is a producer of knowledge Possesses understanding & acceptance of self	Advocacy for new directions & increasing independence Feedback about strengths & possibilities Facilitation of continuing growth Support for risk-taking Ongoing facilitative relationships	Allow development of long-term, integrated plan of study Remove time & space restrictions Develop multiple, related in-depth studies, including mentorships Wide variety of accelerated options Waive traditional school policies & regulations Listen Stay out of their way

Adapted from Neihart, M., & Betts, G. (2010). *Revised profiles of the gifted and talented.*

This chapter has provided a framework to consider social and emotional learning and potential areas of concern for high-ability learners within each area. Ultimately, teachers are not trained counsellors, social workers, or psychologists and when we see behaviours that are concerning and may place the student at risk, then we need to follow the policies and procedures as stipulated by the school and school system. We need to recognize our limits and ensure boundaries are in place. However, the importance of developing a trusting relationship so the student can work through some of these issues cannot be underestimated. Regular one-on-one discussions, formal and informal, together with goal setting can be of great help for a student to feel understood and that they are not facing these problems alone. Social and emotional learning is part of the curriculum and using our knowledge of where high-ability students may need additional support will help ensure they too can develop the skills and knowledge that are essential to thrive as a young person and adult.

Chapter Reflection

- Reflect on a child you feel is gifted, and identify some of their social emotional characteristics. What are some strategies you could use to support them?
- Why is social emotional development relevant to talent development?
- How does your school currently teach social and emotional competence? How does it address the CASEL framework?

Notes

1 Collaborative for Academic Social and Emotional Learning (CASEL). (2023a). *Fundamentals of SEL*. Retrieved 23 January from https://casel.org/fundamentals-of-sel/
2 Olszewski-Kubilius, P., Subotnik, R. F., Davis, L. C., & Worrell, F. C. (2019). Benchmarking psychosocial skills important for talent development. *New Directions for Child and Adolescent Development*, *2019*(168), 161–176.
3 Australian Curriculum Assessment and Reporting Authority. (n.d.). *Personal and Social Capability (Version 8.4)*. Retrieved 23 January from https://australiancurriculum.edu.au/f-10-curriculum/general-capabilities/personal-and-social-capability/

4   Collaborative for Academic Social and Emotional Learning (CASEL). (2023b). *What is the CASEL framework?* Retrieved 23 January from https://casel.org/fundamentals-of-sel/what-is-the-casel-framework/#responsible

5   Ibid.

6   Davis, G. A., Rimm, S. B., & Siegle, D. (2011). *Education of the gifted and talented* (6th ed.). Pearson.

7   Frost, R. O., Marten, P., Lahart, C., & Rosenblate, R. (1990). The dimensions of perfectionism. *Cognitive Therapy and Research, 14*(5), 449–468. https://doi.org/10.1007/BF01172967

8   Ibid.

9   CAPS Counseling and Psychological Services. (2023). *Perfectionistic thinking and behavior.* University of Michigan. https://caps.umich.edu/content/perfectionistic-thinking-and-behavior

10 National Association for Gifted Children. (n.d.). *Perfectionism.* https://www.nagc.org/resources-publications/resources-parents/social-emotional-issues/perfectionism

11 Kornblum, M., & Ainley, M. (2005). Perfectionism and the gifted: A study of an Australian school sample. *International Education Journal, 6.*

12 Nugent, S. A. (2000). Perfectionism: Its manifestations and classroom-based interventions. *Journal of Secondary Gifted Education, 11*(4), 215–221.

13 National Association for Gifted Children. (n.d.). *Perfectionism.* https://www.nagc.org/resources-publications/resources-parents/social-emotional-issues/perfectionism

14 Zakreski, M. J. (2018). When Emotional Intensity and Cognitive Rigidity Collide: What Can Counselors and Teachers Do? *Gifted Child Today, 41*(4), 208–216. https://doi.org/10.1177/1076217518786984

15 Silverman, L. K. (1994). The moral sensitivity of gifted children and the evolution of society. *Roeper Review, 17*(2), 110–116. https://doi.org/10.1080/02783199409553636

16 Gallagher, S. (2022). Openness to experience and overexcitabilities in a sample of highly gifted middle school students. *Gifted Education International, 38*(2), 194–228. https://doi.org/10.1177/02614294211053283

17 Rinn, A. N., & Majority, K. L. (2018). The social and emotional world of the gifted. In *Handbook of giftedness in children* (pp. 49–63). Springer.

18 Gross, M. U. M. (1989). The pursuit of excellence or the search for intimacy? The forced-choice dilemma of gifted youth. *Roeper Review, 11*(4), 189–194.

19 Ibid.

20 Davidson Institute. (2021). *Gifted friendships: Age mate versus true peer.* Davidson Institute,. https://www.davidsongifted.org/gifted-blog/gifted-friendships-age-mate-vs-true-peer/

21 Rogers, K. B. (2007). Lessons learned about educating the Gifted and Talented: A synthesis of the research on educational practice. *Gifted Child Quarterly, 51*(4), 382–396.

22 Fang, J., Huang, X., Zhang, M., Huang, F., Li, Z., & Yuan, Q. (2018). The big-fish-little-pond effect on academic self-concept: A meta-analysis. *Frontiers in psychology, 9*, 1569.

23 Schwabe, F., Korthals, R., & Schils, T. (2019). Positive social relationships with peers and teachers as moderators of the Big-Fish-Little-Pond Effect. *Learning and Individual Differences, 70*, 21–29. https://doi.org/10.1016/j.lindif.2018.12.006

24 Gilbert, W., Guay, F., & Morin, A. J. S. (2022). Can teachers' need-supportive practices moderate the big-fish-little-pond effect? A quasi-experimental study with elementary school children. *Contemp Educ Psychol, 69*, 102060. https://doi.org/10.1016/j.cedpsych.2022.102060

25 Jung, J. Y. (2019). The Career Development of Gifted Students. In J. A. Athanasou & H. N. Perera (Eds.), *International Handbook of Career Guidance* (pp. 325–342). Springer International Publishing. https://doi.org/10.1007/978-3-030-25153-6_15

26 Catholic Education Commission of Victoria. (2018). *CECV Positive behaviour guidelines*. Catholic Education Commission of Victoria.

27 Betts, G. T., & Neihart, M. (1988). Profiles of the Gifted and Talented. *Gifted Child Quarterly, 32*(2), 248–253. https://doi.org/10.1177/001698628803200202

28 Neihart, M., & Betts, G. (2010). *Revised profiles of the gifted and talented.* https://docs.google.com/viewer?a=v&pid=sites&srcid=c3Rqb3NlcGhzLmNvLm56fHN0LWpvc2VwaClzLWNhdGhvbGljLXNjaG9vbC1wdWVtla29oZS1nYXRlfGd4OjVkZWVkNmQ5YjljMzJjYmE

Working with Families

BACK TO BASICS

The home-school partnership is recognized as being highly valued. However, when it comes to gifted students, schools can be dismissive of the claims of parents advocating for their gifted child, and parents can feel uncomfortable approaching teachers worried about being typecast as 'demanding'. This chapter discusses six types of parental involvement schools can draw on to strengthen the partnership.

TAKING IT FURTHER

A selection of practical ways parents can support their high-potential child is provided.

There can be a cynicism amongst some educators (certainly not all) that parents think their child or children are gifted, with unrealistic expectations about what their child can achieve resulting in 'pushy' demands. In my experience, this cannot be further from the truth. In many instances, parents have underestimated their child's ability, or remained quiet because they didn't want to be seen as being 'that parent' or know what support or interventions to ask for. I recall many a parent information session where attendees seemed embarrassed coming along and qualified their attendance with, 'I don't think my child's gifted, I'm just interested in the topic'. Parents have cried at these sessions, as they realized they had a child they now realized had high ability/ ies, but it had gone unrecognized and unsupported.

DOI: 10.4324/9781003267973-6

Once a child starts school, most of their waking time is spent with teachers, generally in a structured environment. What is learnt, how it is learnt, and when it is learnt are largely determined by the teacher. As highlighted in Chapter 2, there can be a lot to be learnt from parents and carers about their high-ability children. Children who present in the classroom as distracted or distracting, disengaged, and unmotivated may get home and transform into motivated, curious, and focused learners. The difference is the environment and not having the constraints that are imposed by the current nature of schooling. And then there may be the children who at school mask their high abilities as a compromise for fitting in with their peers. They may do enough to be what is considered a 'good' student, but the depth of their talents is only on display at home, as she in engrossed in above-level maths content she has sourced from an older sibling, online, or through her parents. And what about the student in Year 2 who learns binary at the dinner table one evening? Or the Year 6 student who builds her own computer on the weekend?

Working with parents and carers is not only good practice, but an essential practice. We saw in Chapter 2 how parents are vital in the identification process, but they are also key partners when it comes to differentiation and talent development itself. Reflecting back on the theories introduced in Chapter 1, they all highlight the role of the family and the environment in talent development. Whilst teachers need to be intentional in meeting the needs of high-ability students, it can be argued that teachers also consider how they work with families to support them in meeting their child's needs. We do this with learners who need additional support who may be below the expected level, so it makes sense that we provide the other end of the bell curve with the same. We do this through involving parents and families.

Six types of parental involvement

The home-school partnership is recognized as an important connection that focuses on students' development and well-being and breaks down the false dichotomy between home and school learning. There are established links between strong partnerships with families and schools as the responsibility for the child's development is seen as a shared endeavour. This is true for all children, regardless of background, ability, and for high-ability/gifted students there are some ways teachers can tap into and use this partnership effectively.

There are six ways that schools can involve parents and families to develop partnerships[1]:

1. Parenting
2. Communicating
3. Volunteering
4. Learning at home
5. Decision making
6. Collaborating with the community

Parenting

Whilst the title of this type of parental involvement may seem jarring, there is most definitely a place for this when working with high-ability/gifted children. And, it's something that is already done in many schools annually. Consider the information nights conducted at the start of the school year where expectations and suggested practices (homework, reading) are shared with families. Schools often offer evenings with guest speakers on topics such as puberty, raising adolescents, cyber safety, etc. Ultimately, this type of connection is about sharing knowledge and understandings with parents to support students in their home environment.

From a Gifted Education perspective, this may take the form of information sessions, online resources, or a series of workshops that tap into a range of topics identified at the local level as being of particular relevance. However, informed by research[2], and through working with families and children, the following understandings seem to be essential. Appendix D provides some key points that can be used and adapted for sharing with parents for each of these:

1. What it means to be gifted/talented
2. How to advocate for their child
3. How to support their child's social/emotional needs
4. How to support their child's talent development

Early intervention and identification of gifted children assists parents and carers in advocating for their children in both formal and informal educational settings. Providing access to this type of information is important as many families are left floundering, unsure of what to do and how to go about doing it. There are groups on social media that can provide answers to some of the parents' questions, but not all are relevant to the Australian system. There are also educational consultants that families may tap into to assist with advocacy, which comes with a cost. Providing information directly to families can address some of the access issues to this sort of information. Of course, there may still be some barriers faced by families when scheduling workshops or information sessions. For example, when sessions are held during the day, participation is restricted to those who do not have work commitments, and evenings may rule out shift workers or those who have young children, or managing a family schedule filled with out of school hours activities.

Given these sessions are 'opt-in', there may be families who would benefit from attending but may choose not to. This may be for any number of reasons, including those who may feel uncomfortable making a public declaration (through attendance) that they think their child is gifted or high potential, or may not recognize their child's abilities as being anything other than normal. Parents' field of reference about their child and their interests and abilities will depend on the size of their family, social networks, educational and care settings. A comment from parents that I have heard many times is that they don't notice anything exceptional about their child, they are just their child.

Ways of increasing access to this information include:

1. Recording any in-person workshops
2. Offering online webinars
3. Sharing any presentation materials via the school's website or platform
4. Having materials prepared in different languages relevant to your school community
5. Sharing the development and facilitation of these sessions across local schools in area/region

Communicating

> For families and students to feel supported ensure 'regular communications with the families about the child's progress'
>
> – Sally (parent)

All teachers know that communication between schools and families is an essential element across all aspects of a child's education and well-being. But when working with students and families who may require more distinct types of interventions, such as withdrawal programs or acceleration, communication (what, how, why, and with whom) must be considered from the outset. Teachers are busy, and families are busy and the amount of communications that are often one-way (from school to home) can be overwhelming. Emails now tend to replace paper notices or learning management systems send out notifications, but regardless of the mode, there is a lot of information for families to process and keep on top of. Determining what needs to be communicated and the most effective way, or ways, of communicating, recognizing that communication is minimum two-way, will ensure that important details about a student's progress and how their learning needs are being met are known and understood by all. It is crucial that families are kept informed about what is being done, why it is being done and to seek their input and feedback on this. As noted, parents know their child in ways that teachers will not and using this expertise can expedite the implementation of appropriate interventions and ways of working with the child.

Communication isn't just restricted to the families of high-ability students. There can be reluctance to discuss the provisions that may be in place for these students, perhaps stemming from concern that other families or students may feel that they are missing out, or that it isn't relevant. However, classrooms do not operate within a vacuum and students will share with their families if a classmate is heading off to a 'fun' group activity whilst they remain in the classroom. Or parents may discuss the different things their child is doing at school. And whilst individual differentiation is not something that should ever be shared with other families, it is important that educational experiences that look like 'fun' are not kept secret. Rather, it can be helpful if the school community is aware why these learning opportunities, designed specifically to meet the needs of high-ability students, and possibly involve withdrawal from usual classroom schedules or meet outside of class time, are available to certain students and not to others. (This assumes, of course, that the nature of the planned experiences is inappropriate for all students.) It is reasonable and valid for parents and carers to have questions about why their child is not able to participate in these activities, particularly if the child has expressed an interest in the focus of the experience. It is best to engage with families to learn more about the child. Identification of gifted or high-ability learners, as we know, can be difficult in schools for a whole range of reasons. And if a parent suggests that certain activities may be suited for their child, teachers can discover a learner's abilities in areas in which they were previously unaware. Of course, this won't always be the case. It is natural for parents and carers to want the best for their child and to have access to opportunities that others have. In my experience, when parents do ask the question about inclusion and I describe the nature of the learning (pace, content, etc.), nine times out of ten parents will acknowledge that it's not the best learning environment for their child. In cases where parents continue to strongly advocate for their child's inclusion, and in the absence of glaringly obvious reasons to not include them, I recommend giving the child a go. If the child agrees, allow them to join the activity or experience. Students are very good at recognizing when they feel uncomfortable and out of their depth. As long as the learner has a way of communicating with their family and/or teacher honestly about their 'fit' with the group, then there is no reason to not give them an opportunity.

Communication involves more than just sharing what happens and the decisions that are being made at school with families. The two- or many-way communication that occurs from school to family, family to school, learner to school and family, etc. also includes learner progress. The traditional model of twice-yearly reports and interviews or three-way conferences (student, family, teacher) to the increasingly common continuous reporting model ensures that progress across curriculum-based disciplines is shared and understood. But what about if students are being provided additional learning interventions through withdrawal or pull-out programs or are part of extra-curricular activities outside of class hours. How will the learning that takes place during these experiences be communicated with the learner and their families? And who is responsible for the reporting? When students are removed from their usual timetabled lessons, whether it be a primary classroom or a secondary school subject, to a withdrawal program, there should be planned learning intentions and goals shaping this program. What the students learn by the end of the program should be clearly communicated with students and families prior to the commencement of any such program, as well as the process and timing for communicating learner progress on these learning goals. When and how this is communicated will depend on individual school systems and processes, as well as the duration and nature of the program. Some examples of programs and associated reporting are shown in Table 6.1.

When families feel comfortable communicating with teachers, information that is important for schools to know about how students are going or concerns at home can be more readily shared, facilitating appropriate actions

Table 6.1 Programs and ways of communicating student progress

Program name	Description	Duration	Reporting
Reading Prep – Year 3	Multi-age primary school-based withdrawal reading program, children selected book from a curated list and engage in a range of text analysis activities	Year-long	Written report provided twice yearly (June, December) as part of the school report, teacher was available for scheduled parent-teacher interviews (mid-year) as well as inviting parents to meet at any time to discuss progress
Year 7 Maths	Year 7 withdrawal program drawing on the Australian Mathematics Trust MCYA Enrichment program, APSMO Olympiads, and an investigative unit	Year-long	Mid-year student-led 3-way conference. Students prepared a reflective PowerPoint presentation, selecting work samples describing how they felt at the start, their responses and strategies while working through the sample, and how they felt and what they learned once completed. Students set goals for the remaining semester and reflected on how they have grown as a learner through their experience in the program. For end of year, a written report was provided as part of the school report
Interschool design thinking challenge	Students were grouped across schools and relied on digital collaborative tools to work together to develop a prototype	Semester	Written report provided at the time of school-based reporting cycle. An exhibition of all projects was conducted after school hours to provide parents/families with opportunity to see and engage with the finished prototype
Design thinking project	Students identified a problem and worked through the design thinking steps to develop a solution and prototype	Semester	Digital portfolio of selected work samples based on general capabilities and design thinking process. For example, selecting evidence or describing how well they collaborated with their team. Shared with parents through digital access

and/or support. Ensuring appropriate and effective communication with families circumvents many issues from arising.

Volunteering

Involving parents through volunteering in school-related activities is an interesting space given the changing nature of families and workforce participation. According to 2022 Australian labour force statistics, 74.7% of couple families with school-aged children have a mother that works, while 68.7% of all one-parent families are employed[3]. This impacts the ways in which families can volunteer and help with programs or experiences offered within the school.

In primary schools, parent volunteering is often limited to helping with reading groups, attending excursions and/or camps, or perhaps working in a canteen. In secondary schools, the opportunities for parent volunteers are limited even further. The role of parent volunteers in school councils, committees, or cultural groups is important and indeed necessary for schools. But broadening the scope and ways in which volunteers are utilized in schools is one way of enriching the experiences schools can offer all students.

The easiest way to gauge how families' expertise can be used in schools is to ask. Expertise, interest, and availability can all be ascertained through a quick online survey using freely available software like Google Forms, Survey Monkey, etc. Using a short questionnaire, schools can create a database of parents, carers, and extended family who are interested in volunteering. Asking open questions about areas of expertise and interest, availability, preferred frequency, and age groups will allow for all families to share their talents that can then be incorporated across the whole school, as well as being available for high-ability educational experiences. An example of this is working with a grandparent of a family who was a retired aeronautical engineer. He worked with students on a fortnightly basis for a term. The students continued to work through the activities he provided on the alternate week and checked their understandings upon his return.

In some instances, parents may be able to take on programs that can be conducted after school. Competitions such as Tournament of Minds and the Future Problem Solving Program don't need to have a trained teacher to facilitate them. Or perhaps they may take on a mentoring role with a group of students.

Of course, all volunteers need to be assessed for suitability prior to commencing any work with the school. Once they commence, induction and training need to be provided for the volunteer about child safety, confidentiality, and school processes as guided by a school's volunteer policy.

Learning at home

Learning at home is a contentious issue, with some schools having a 'no homework' policy, others setting family-based activities as homework, and yet others who have a clear policy about how many hours per night according to grade level. The debates about the merits of homework at primary versus secondary school are beyond the scope of this discussion. Ultimately, how learning at home occurs within each school setting will be determined by the policy of the school, informed by the jurisdictional guidelines.

For all students, and especially for high-ability students, there is a risk that homework will become 'busy work'. Any learning at home needs to be have a focus on quality rather than quantity. Homework can create tension at home between parents and children, so when offering opportunities for parent involvement through this channel, it becomes important to get it right. A parent told the story of her high-ability primary school-aged child refusing to complete the homework task set by the classroom teacher. Wanting to support the school, the parent described a frustrating week of trying different persuasive techniques to support the school. In the end, the child was willing to accept the punishments from both home and school. When asked why there was so much resistance to the task, the child explained that it was seen as an art and craft activity that had no real purpose, other than taking up their time that could be spent on other things.

Throughout the year, it's not uncommon for schools to include articles in newsletters or similar that discuss the things parents can do with their children to support their learning. For primary school students, these suggestions might include using card games to help with counting, pointing out mathematical concepts in real life, or calculating how much change is expected when shopping. The same thing can be provided for high-ability students. Whilst parents are experts on their child, they may struggle to know how to provide enriching home learning experiences for their child. Providing no-cost and low-cost options will assist with accessibility, as well as consideration for time parents and children have available given other demands on their time. There are many free educational websites that provide online courses (e.g., Khan Academy), lessons or investigations (e.g., NRich from University of Cambridge), or providing opportunities for passion projects.

Low-cost strategy board games such as Connect 4 or Roadblock to the Catan series also provide ways of engaging families with learning. Parents may not know of games that would be suitable for their child, so these suggestions always seem to be appreciated. Offering up similar ideas about ways to extend a child's learning in an area of interest, or expose them to potential new interests, is another valuable way of linking parents into learning at home activities (e.g., going to a museum, art gallery, or significant cultural/historic sites). However, this information doesn't just need to be about types of learning at home. It can also take the shape of sharing strategies to support students with homework tasks such as helping with time management, perfectionism, getting started, or organizing ideas.

Often learning at home, particularly in the early years of schooling, involves families through daily home reading. Other times the homework may be a set of Maths problems or spelling words. When parents are involved with learning at home, they can become partners in making sure the activities are contributing to the child's learning in a positive way. This type of 'practice' homework should reflect the learning outcomes and reinforce the learning at school. As previously discussed, (see Chapter 3), there is no point setting homework that is below the child's current level of skill and understandings. It is important that students, and families, know the connection between the learning in the classroom and the learning at home that has been set.

Decision making

It is established practice in Australian schools that parents are active members on school councils or boards and associated committees who make myriad decisions to keep the school functioning and safe. In addition to the school council, schools may also have a Parents' Association or Club that is focused more on supporting the school community and establishing a sense of community.

An additional way of providing an avenue for parents to be involved is through the formation of groups with a specific focus. Over time, I learnt that parents felt ill-equipped in how to support and advocate for their high-ability/gifted child. The conversations between families during information sessions led to the development of a parent group that focused on supporting high-ability children. This group was designed to be an advocacy group of sorts to learn more about Gifted Education and ways to support high-potential learners. It was advertised and open to any parent in the school who was interested in the field. The meetings were facilitated by a Gifted Education teacher and at the time were offered during the day. The first thing the group did was for each attendee to answer the following questions:

1. What do you hope this group will achieve both short term (this year) and long term?
2. What are some ways/resources to achieve these goals?
3. What would you like to see happen in terms of Gifted Education? (e.g., guest speakers for students, parents)
4. It is important that we establish a charter and protocols so that all members understand the guiding principles of our team. What are some suggestions to be included in this? (including dissemination of information, wider school community communication/involvement, roles within group)

Ideas that were generated and brought to fruition included coordinating volunteers to work with groups of students, reintroducing a Chess Club on Friday afternoons (primary school) and establishing a wiki (cutting edge technology at the time!) where useful resources and information about school offerings could be stored and shared. Over time, as satisfaction levels increased, interest waned, and the group eventually dissolved. Those involved saw how their involvement led to positive changes that were not onerous at all.

Collaborating with the community

When schools collaborate with external community resources and services, parents become aware of the types of resources and support that are available to them in their local community. There are many ways that schools can, and do, collaborate with community including social service events (e.g., the school choir attending an aged-care home or volunteering at Australian Disability Enterprises or sheltered workshops), participation in tree planting days with 'Friends of' environmental groups, or connecting with a local charity to collect donations or taking part in hands-on workshops.

Drawing on the resources in the community means tapping into the financial, social, material, and economic resources that will provide positive outcomes for students and families not just while at school but will have a lasting impact as well. Examples of how this might be done with high-ability students in mind is:

- Using alumni to work with current students in their area of expertise. For example, employing a university student alum to teach high-ability students high-level mathematics
- Connecting with tertiary institutions school outreach programs, or asking for PhD or research students to act as mentors/experts to assist with a topic or project
- Asking academics or experts to speak with students or conduct a workshop on an issue
- Partnering with businesses to develop practical solutions to tackle real-life problem the business is facing
- Connecting with health and well-being services to provide information and advice on issues common amongst high-ability students (e.g., perfectionism)
- Connecting with volunteer organizations such as UN Youth Australia to volunteer or participate in the many events on offer.

Taking it further

The role of parents in talent development

Working in partnership with parents is essential for all learners. For non-gifted, mainstream students, parents generally have ready access to ways in which they can support their child's learning and development. However, once a child's learning needs become qualitatively and quantitatively different to most of their chronological peers, parents can feel lost and unsure of how best to support their child. There are several websites and groups on social media where parents can find a global online community where similar problems, experiences are shared and discussed. There is also local state-based gifted and talented associations and international associations such as the American National Association for Gifted Children (NAGC) that provide information (although not everything on the NAGC is relevant for an Australian setting).

As parents, we should be SUPPORTIVE when a child expresses his/her interest in something; GUIDE them and be part of their achievements
— Kenny (parent)

A selection of things parents can do to support their high-potential child is listed in Box 6.1[4,5]. This is not an exhaustive list but is a starting point that can be shared with parents.

Box 6.1 Ways parents can support their high-ability child

1. Expose your child to new experiences that may spark an interest and arouse curiosity
2. Encourage a growth mindset – celebrate success but be sure to encourage taking learning risks even if this results in failure or lower than usual marks
3. Seek out a group of like-minded peers for your child based on common interests, these may be based on cognitive age rather than chronological
4. Acknowledge and support your child's interests, e.g., taking them to a library to borrow books in a topic, taking them to an exhibition at a museum, art gallery
5. Engage and encourage curiosity by answering questions, or helping them find the answer
6. Encourage a balance between study and relaxation
7. Manage or keep an eye on their commitments. Many interests may lead to too many commitments
8. If seeing signs of unhealthy perfectionism (stress, risk avoidance, procrastination), you can help by:
   - Normalizing and modelling mistakes
   - Focusing on growth rather than results
   - Appreciate attempts instead of outcomes
   - Focus on process instead of result
   - Help with chunking tasks into smaller, more manageable segments and attach a timeline

9. Recognize that your child's development is asynchronous – they may be cognitively advanced for their age, but social and emotional development may be at a much lower level
10. Gifted children can be very sensitive and very observant. They may respond strongly to social justice issues or local/world events. Discuss concerns with your child and look for ways to help them manage this. It may be through action such as organizing care packages after a natural disaster
11. Discuss your child's learning needs with them. Acknowledge their abilities and guide them in ways they can advocate for themselves
12. Advocate for your child. If you know their learning needs are not being met, speak with the teacher and focus on the child's learning needs and how they might be met

Summary

This chapter has described the ways in which schools and teachers can work with parents of high-ability learners. Working with parents and families can create better outcomes for students, individually and collectively. There will be restrictions as to what can realistically be done given staffing, resources, etc. Determine and prioritize what will have maximum impact given the available resources. Taking any opportunity to develop positive relationships with families will strengthen the home-school partnership.

Chapter Reflection

- What are the ways in which your school currently works with parents of gifted students?
- What might be some of the barriers to parental involvement in your school? How might you address these barriers?
- What are some short-term goals for strengthening these partnerships?
- What are some long-term goals for strengthening these partnerships?

Notes

1 Epstein, J. L., Greenfield, M. D., Sanders, M. G., Sheldon, S., Simon, B. S., Salinas, K. C., Jansorn, N. R., VanVoorhis, F. L., Martin, C. S., & Thomas, B. G. (2018). *School, family, and community partnerships: Your handbook for action.* Corwin Press. http://ebookcentral.proquest.com/lib/latrobe/detail.action?docID=6261801

2 Olszewski-Kubilius, P. (2018). The Role of the Family in Talent Development. In S. I. Pfeiffer (Ed.), *Handbook of Giftedness in Children: Psychoeducational Theory, Research, and Best Practices* (pp. 129–147). Springer International Publishing. https://doi.org/10.1007/978-3-319-77004-8_9

3 Australian Bureau of Statistics. (2022). *Labour force status of families: Explores how fammiles engage with the labour market.* https://www.abs.gov.au/statistics/labour/employment-and-unemployment/labour-force-status-families/latest-release#key-statistics

4 Olszewski-Kubilius, P. (2018). The Role of the Family in Talent Development. In S. I. Pfeiffer (Ed.), *Handbook of Giftedness in Children: Psychoeducational Theory, Research, and Best Practices* (pp. 129–147). Springer International Publishing. https://doi.org/10.1007/978-3-319-77004-8_9

5 National Association for Gifted Children. (n.d.). *Perfectionism.* http://www.nagc.org/sites/default/files/Publication%20PHP/NAGC-TIP%20Sheet-Perfectionism-FINAL_0.pdf

APPENDIX D: HELPFUL HINTS FOR PARENTS

1. **What it means to be gifted/talented**

   High potential/high ability can be defined in many ways. Generally, when talking about high ability, we are talking about students who have the capacity to learn rapidly, and may display a range of characteristics such as emotional intensity, moral sensitivity, deep thinking, and advanced vocabulary. Gifted students may have interests that are not typical for their age, have an adult-like sense of humour, and have an easier time talking with adults or older children than their age-mates.

   The ability to learn quickly and easily may lead to feelings of frustration in classrooms where their leaning needs are not being met.

2. **How to advocate for their child**

   - Recognize your role in advocating for your child – if you don't do it, who will?

- Form a relationship with the class or pastoral/homeroom teacher, this may be through regular check-ins (email, phone calls)
- Seek to understand what is happening at school for your child. The best place to start is with the class or pastoral/homeroom teacher
- Be clear about what you want to discuss or the outcome(s) you are looking for. Focusing on one or two issues or concerns
- Make a time to meet. Five minutes before the bell is not ideal.
- Research – become informed about different options or solutions that you can bring to the discussion. Teachers do not always have the answers, and want to do their best for all students, so working in partnership with a teacher is a positive way forward
- Ask for follow-up meetings to review any interventions stemming from the meeting

3. **How to support their child's social emotional needs**

High-ability or gifted children may not follow typical rates of development in areas such as intellectual, social emotional, and physical development. This is referred to as asynchronous development and it can be confusing for the child, parents, teachers, and peers.

Ways of supporting a child's social emotional needs that may stem from asynchronous development are:

- Listen, provide opportunities for to decompress
- Focus on strengths
- Encourage a balance between study and relaxation (what does downtime look like?)
- Emphasizing effort rather than the result
- Help develop positive self-talk
- Discuss difference between excellence and perfection
- Bibliotherapy (using stories to address affective needs). (*'Some of my best friends are books'* by Judith Halsted provides a list of books addressing a range of issues grouped by age)
- Gifted children can be very sensitive and very observant. They may respond strongly to social justice issues or local/world events. Discuss concerns with your child and look for ways to help them manage this. It may be through action such as organizing care packages after a natural disaster
- Provide safe opportunities to take risks
- Provide opportunities to be with like-minded peers (may be interest, rather than age-based)

- Help develop timelines, break tasks down into manageable tasks and recognition of when less precision is okay.

4. **How to support their child's talent development**

- Expose your child to new experiences that may spark an interest and arouse curiosity
- Encourage a growth mindset – celebrate success but be sure to encourage taking learning risks even if this results in failure or lower than usual marks
- Seek out a group of like-minded peers for your child based on common interests, these may be based on cognitive age rather than chronological
- Acknowledge and support your child's interests, e.g., taking them to a library to borrow books in a topic, taking them to an exhibition at a museum, art gallery
- Engage and encourage curiosity by answering questions, or helping them find the answer
- Manage or keep an eye on their commitments. Many interests may lead to too many commitments
- If seeing signs of unhealthy perfectionism (stress, risk avoidance, procrastination), you can help by:
  - Normalizing and modelling mistakes
  - Focusing on growth rather than results
  - Appreciate attempts instead of outcomes
  - Focus on process instead of result
  - Help with chunking tasks into smaller, more manageable segments and attach a timeline
- Recognize that your child's development is asynchronous – they may be cognitively advanced for their age, but social and emotional development may be at a much lower level
- Discuss your child's learning needs with them. Acknowledge their abilities and guide them in ways they can advocate for themselves
- Advocate for your child. If you know their learning needs are not being met, speak with the teacher and focus on the child's learning needs and how they might be met

Collaboration, Partnerships, and Networks

7

BACK TO BASICS

Often, teachers who work in Gifted Education are working in isolation in their schools. This may be a specialized role, or an additional leadership position. This chapter identifies the ways in which we can enhance and strengthen our school practices through establishing communities of practice with colleagues from other schools. Partnerships with external organizations provide expertise and mentoring opportunities to benefit our gifted learners. This section offers a template that can be used to plan a mentoring program for students.

TAKING IT FURTHER

As the concluding chapter of this book, a helpful and practical way of moving forward as a school is to develop a Gifted Education policy that brings together the understandings covered in the preceding chapters. A template and suggested process for policy development is provided.

It can feel isolating for those in schools who have the responsibility of overseeing or coordinating high-ability or high-potential programs in their school. This may be exacerbated if there has not been any formal training in this area and trying to learn as you go. When I first began in the field, I was reading anything I could get access to online and searching for as much professional learning as I could. Unfortunately, in Victoria at the time, there was not a lot available. So I contacted our school's Department of Education

DOI: 10.4324/9781003267973

Table 7.1 Key characteristics of communities of practice

Dimension	Description
Purpose	To develop capacity of members through building and exchanging knowledge, understandings, and practice
Membership	Self-selected group of peers who opt in due to interest and need
Sustainability	Group is sustained through perceived value by members (linked to passion, commitment, and group's expertise)
Duration	As long as necessary or there is interest

Regional Office and, in collaboration with them, organized a couple of full-day sessions with an experienced academic for teachers in the region.

Whilst one-off professional learning opportunities can be beneficial, collaboration with colleagues on shared goals can strengthen and improve capacity for all members of the group. This is the power of communities of practice. Communities of practice are not new, with jurisdictions such as Victoria transforming a previous network model and adopting a Community of Practice approach to guide and drive learning and impact at local school level[1].

Community of practice and networks

Communities of practice (CoP) do not need to be a long-term, high-commitment proposition. Rather, they will continue for as long as the members find it useful. The key aspects of a community of practice[2] are described in Table 7.1. Rather than being a mandated group, overseen by school leadership or management, this group can be initiated by any interested, motivated staff member and established in a way that meets all members' needs.

It is important to make the distinction between what may be referred to as a network and a community of practice. Both have utility but will likely serve different purposes. As with CoP, a network may be set up formally or informally by a group of interested members from across different schools or initiated by associations with the aim of recruiting those interested in the topic/focus. But a network's purpose will not solely be on improving members' capacity and understanding of working with high-ability students.

When establishing a successful education-focused CoP[3]:

1. Gather a core group of colleagues who are passionate about Gifted Education and serving high-ability learners.

2. Have a clear purpose for the group. The example above didn't set out to solve a specific problem such as identification, rather, the goal was more broadly about improving members' understandings and practice across a range of practice-based topics.

3. Begin with a problem-oriented task or project. The group began with the question of how to identify high-ability learners where practical strategies that had been trialled in schools were shared and challenged.

4. Maintain openness in the CoP, this includes membership. As news of the CoP success spreads, more staff in other schools may want to join. This will bring new perspectives. New members may come and go and bring variable levels of commitment.

5. Consider reaching out to invite knowledgeable 'experts' and 'innovators' to join.

6. A facilitator is useful in coordinating the group and building connections within the group. A 'driver' of the group will maintain and sustain the group for longer, ensuring the group remains relevant and connected.

7. Ensure the CoP is of benefit to the members, adding value to their work and meeting the needs of the core group.

8. Support from schools to assist the CoP will improve the outcomes for all members as well as prolonging the longevity of the CoP. Ideally, time for the CoP will be built in and/or recognized as an appropriate alternative for what may be scheduled at that time.

9. Sustaining the CoP over time will depend on its value as perceived by its members. It needs to be meeting the needs of the group and translating into improved practice.

10. Share the successes of the CoP with whoever will listen! This will not only spread the word to attract new members, but also validate and potentially spread the work of the members.

11. Consider various formats and locations for the CoP. Meeting online removes geographical barriers (assuming internet connection is available), particularly for rural settings, and removes additional travel time that extends the working day.

12. Consider ways of evaluating the CoP by identifying the ways members' practices have changed and the effect of these changes. Identifying this serves a number of purposes, including contributing to members' annual performance and development reviews, identifying areas for improvement and the ways in which the CoP has benefitted them.

Ultimately, the CoP needs to work for the core members involved. However, whenever, wherever, and for how long members come together can be determined by the group to suit their own context.

Community of practice: A case study

Where the network examples illustrate how schools can work together to provide many and varied opportunities to work with like-minded peers for high-ability students, this example focuses on how the network model can be tweaked to form a community of practice.

Through conversations with colleagues, a primary teacher determined there was a want and need for a community of practice focusing on high-ability students and ways to provide appropriate educational experiences. An invitation to connect was distributed via email to neighbouring schools and through existing connections and included schools from all sectors (government, Catholic, and independent). The invitation set out clearly the intended aims of the CoP. It was to be a forum for us to share expertise, ask questions, share practice, bounce ideas around, and to support each other in raising the profile of these learners in our schools. There was no leader appointed, rather it was a space where all members shaped the content and direction of our meetings based on need and/or interest. However, there was undoubtedly a 'driver' who maintained momentum when required. Hosting duties were shared amongst members, with the host responsible for sharing an agenda and taking minutes.

The contexts of the schools were similar, but still unique. Expertise ranged from those with a burgeoning interest to others with 25 years plus working with high-ability students. The group was characterized by the supportive and collegial relationship between all members.

Networks

Networks are useful in sharing information, providing resources and professional learning. They can serve teachers, schools, parents/carers, and children through a wide range of opportunities and helpful links to additional information or services.

These networks may be in the form of associations, such as the Australian Association for the Education of the Gifted and Talented or any of Australia's state-based associations. Most Australian states have a dedicated Gifted and Talented association, apart from Northern Territory and Queensland (at the time of writing). All of these associations offer professional learning for schools or individual teachers, and, to varying degrees, provide families and students with workshops and resources. There is a membership fee to join the relevant association, with fees ranging from as low as $25 for an individual to $66. School and organization memberships are available at a higher cost, and options for family memberships are financially accessible.

Networks can also be established at a local community level, with teachers in schools establishing their own network. These networks can be useful when developing school-based activities or workshops that can be opened up to other schools or sharing the workload in establishing events. For example, a government primary school teacher was planning a debating unit with a group of high-ability students. Rather than keep the debates to the usual in-house audience, she wanted to provide a more authentic experience for this group of students. She reached out to other government schools in her local area via email to gauge interest from other teachers in participating in the event. The planning and organization were shared amongst those who expressed interest, so everyone felt some ownership of the event. Five schools responded and a representative from each formed a planning team and together they negotiated the details of the event, including number of teams, costs, format of the day, prizes, debate topics, sourcing independent (experienced) adjudicators, etc. Each school was responsible for determining the best ways to prepare their students for the debates. This network of teachers worked well together to get the event up and running, ensuring it was a positive and exciting experience for all participating students. The success of this event motivated this group of teachers to aim to expand the network, and to ensure there was an interschool event that could be held each year for high-ability students.

Another example of a successful local network is one based in Victoria focusing on high school students from Years 7 to 10. This network brings together teachers from independent, Catholic, and government schools and maintains a regular meeting schedule, meeting once per term. Hosting duties are shared amongst school representatives. Whilst membership of this group mainly consisted of those with a Gifted Education specialist role or responsibility of some description, it was open to others as well. Given its geographic location, it was also largely comprised of independent schools. This group was very active in organizing a plethora of student workshops throughout the year, with multiple opportunities available each term. Examples of student activities on offer included single-day events such as poetry slam competitions, maths days, academic challenges, and student forums with academics. Longer term activities included an online and in-person collaborative design thinking project.

Partnerships

Establishing partnerships between schools and other organizations (including other schools) will provide opportunities for high-ability learners that may otherwise be unavailable. This does not mean that these partnerships should be exclusive to an identified group of high-ability learners at the expense of other students. Rather, the work that is done with the high-ability learners and the partner organization should be tailored to the needs of this group. There are a range of organizations that have specific programs in place to tap into for schools to access. For example, the CSIRO facilitates the national volunteer program, STEM Professionals in Schools, a matching service for schools and STEM professionals to connect based on their needs, interests, and availability.

Parents/grandparents and community organizations

Of course, partnerships don't require external organizations, they may be the result of tapping into the skills and experience of parents and grandparents. One way of doing this is putting a call out at some stage during the year to families with an expression of interest in volunteering to work with a group of students, their area of expertise, and their availability (as discussed in Chapter 6). One year, a retired grandfather who held his pilot licence and was an aeronautical engineer worked with a group of students over a term teaching them Aeronautics 101. There are also anecdotes of parents offering their expertise and being refused, possibly out of concern of some underlying motive of the parent (e.g., 'spying' on the teachers). Unless there are valid reasons to not take up these offers, allowing parents in to help in ways that can't otherwise be provided should be embraced.

Student mentors

Tapping into students, current and past, is another way of providing both role models and expertise that may not otherwise be accessible. This may be something that is offered as part of a voluntary, leadership-style program, but, if possible, payment for their expertise provides recognition of the value of their time and expertise. For high schools, this might be done by seeking expressions of interest from alums that have commenced tertiary studies and have expertise in an area, e.g., Maths or coding. For primary schools, the ready access may be a little more difficult given the space of time between students leaving the school, and when they might be ready to participate in a role such as this. However, that will be largely dependent on individual students and their circumstances. Another option for primary schools would be to speak with local high schools and potentially establish a program or seek out potential recently graduated students through contacts or advertizing.

Use of mentors, whether they be students (secondary or tertiary) or adults, requires planning and consideration regarding the goals, format, and targeted students for the mentoring program. The Davidson Institute, an American-based not-for-profit talent development foundation, offers a comprehensive online guide for establishing and conducting mentor programs[4] (see https://www.davidsongifted.org/wp-content/uploads/2021/03/Davidson_Guidebook_Mentoring_2021.pdf). Mentoring programs may be one-on-one, group based, or be conducted online. Each format has its pros and cons and the choice of model will come down to the purpose and what you hope to achieve through offering the mentor program. Time for training the mentor and reviewing the program at various points needs to also be planned for.

Classroom teachers

Collaboration between classroom teachers and those teachers in the schools who have an interest or role in Gifted Education can be powerful and effective. Establishing shared responsibility for the well-being and learning needs of gifted students can lead to better identification practices, programming, and assessment. These partnerships also recognize that the needs of the learner cannot be met by a 'specialist' program alone. These additional opportunities can be considered the icing on the cake, but the day-to-day modifications happen in the classroom. Working together in partnership increases professional learning for all involved, that inevitably flows into regular teacher practice, and benefits all learners.

Planning a mentor program

This section provides a practical template that can be used in planning a mentor program. This is a guide only and can be easily adjusted to suit individual needs.

Mentoring planning proforma

Establishing

1. What is the goal of your mentoring program?
2. How will you identify students that are suitable for the mentoring program?
3. How will you invite these students and communicate with parents before, during, and after the mentoring program?
4. What format will the program take?
   a. One-on-one
   b. Group
   c. Online
   d. Combination: _____
5. How frequently/how many sessions will be offered? For example weekly, fortnightly, check in once a term?
6. What are the characteristics and expertise required in your mentor(s) for this to succeed?
7. How will you source a mentor(s)? How will you select an appropriate mentor?
8. What training is required for the mentor? (e.g., expectations, Child Safe inductions, etc.). Who will provide this training? When and how will it be offered?
9. What resources are required (e.g., rooms, video conferencing, financial, class materials) and are they available to support the program?

Monitoring

1. What does success look like? How will you know if the mentoring program is adding value?
2. Identify appropriate check-points to check in with mentees and mentor(s) about the program.
3. How will progress and student learning be communicated with students and their families?

Concluding

1. What is the anticipated life-span of this mentoring program?
2. How will the program be evaluated?
3. How will this be shared with the school community?
4. What happens to students at the conclusion of the program? Will it lead into additional complementary opportunities?
5. In what ways can the relationship with the mentor be sustained and fostered over time (if appropriate)?

Taking it further

Developing a Gifted Education policy

A useful exercise for schools is to develop a Gifted Education policy. As with all policies, having this document in place will provide guidelines about best practice and enable greater consistency and awareness of how high-ability learners will be catered for in a school. The process of policy development provides an opportunity for professional learning as those involved work through the questions of who, how, when, what, and why. The following section outlines what to include in a Gifted Education policy and a step-by-step process of how this can be developed. This process has been tried and tested and can be modified to suit local school contexts (see Appendix E for a sample policy).

A policy should have a broad aim, such as 'Support the academic outcomes of high potential students', and will describe:

1. Key definitions, rationale and aims, important documents
2. What is to be done (identification, provision, year levels)

3. Who is to do it? How will they be supported in this role? What staff development is required?
4. How is it implemented?
   a. Within class programs and strategies?
   b. Activities beyond the classroom?
   c. Accelerated progression
   d. Organizational issues
   e. Transition and transfer
5. Resources
6. Who is it benefitting?
7. Monitoring and evaluation. What changes are expected? What does success look like?

Beginning with a shared vision

> 'It's an important day in everyone's life when they begin to work for what they want to build rather than to please a boss…Let's create the future we individually and collectively want'[5]

(p. 315–322)

The value of a shared vision cannot be underestimated, and whilst it is inevitable that not everyone will end up in full agreement, policy development teams should be able to capture the essence of the ideal conditions for high-ability learners for their context. The Walk and Talk activity can be used to develop a shared vision.

Walk and talk

Team up with a 'learning partner'. Your task is to envision what teaching and learning would be like in an ideal school, system, or classroom that caters for gifted students. What would it look like? What do you see, hear, feel? Put yourself in the picture. Go for a walk with your partner. One talks for 5 minutes while the other listens hard for underlying beliefs about learning and feeds back what was heard. Reverse the roles of talker and listener. This process is a way to bring to the surface intuitively held beliefs they were not yet articulated. On your return to the staffroom, record on the sentence cards the key ideas from your vision. As a group, attempt to arrange the cards in an order that makes sense and clearly articulates a **shared vision**.

144

Developing a Rationale

A rationale explains the 'why' of the policy. Why does the school need and want to develop a policy for high-ability learners. There may be references to background materials or educational or other factors that led to the development of the policy. This might reflect what you have learnt from reading this book! It is important to recognize that implicit beliefs and attitudes will affect how this policy is developed and the implementation of any provisions. An awareness of high-ability learners' needs and characteristics will inform the reasons why the policy is being developed.

A thinking routine, such as the 1:4:P:C:R (Publish: Circle: Refine), can be useful for this step:

Question: Why are we writing a policy for Gifted Education?

Step 1: Individually write a response for the question above. Create first draft in silence (5–10 mins)

Step 2: Share your ideas with the other three in your group and discuss the different responses (10 minutes)

Step 3: Create a combined response and write this clearly on an A3 sheet of paper using a texta (5–10 mins) **(Publish)**

Step 4: Post the A3 sheet on the wall and leave one person behind as the explainer. The groups of now three move around the room, reading and discussing the contents of the sheets and challenging the explainers. Take notes as you walk around the room.

Step 5: Return to the home group, discuss the notes made and the new understandings generated from circling the room, and discuss ways to improve the published response.

Refine and share with whole group.

Definitions

Establishing agreement on the terms you use (e.g., gifted, talented, high ability, high potential) and how they will be defined is the next step as this will shape the practices outlined throughout the policy. Referring to Chapter 1 and considering the different theoretical models will help with this process.

Principles and procedures of identification

This section will be informed by the theoretical framework the school has decided upon in the previous step. The battery of instruments to be used (see Chapter 2) can be listed here and will provide the defensible principles underpinning the processes.

Staff development

Consider how this will be managed and resourced. How will staff develop their understandings of high-ability learners and develop appropriate educational experiences?

Provision

This section can describe both within class and withdrawal or external opportunities. It can also detail grouping practices that will inform class structures each year (e.g., cluster grouping).

Accelerated progression

Considering how any acceleration progressions will function across the school and having clear processes save a lot of on-the-spot decision making that often has long-term consequences. Well-intentioned, 'spontaneous' acceleration decisions can create issues that prior planning will ameliorate. Clearly detailed expectations and clarification of roles and responsibilities remove ambiguity and confusion.

Organizational issues

As with all facets of school life, things don't just happen. There always needs to be someone overseeing and managing processes and implementation, from staff learning to student programs. Timetabling of withdrawal programs also needs to be considered here.

Transition and Transfer

How will transitions such as starting primary school and high school be managed? What sort of information is collected from pre-schools and kindergartens? How are secondary schools learning about their incoming Year 7s. For example, knowing that early identification means early intervention, are schools asking about whether a Prep/Foundation child is already reading and are they being placed in a class with other early readers?

Resources

Consider what resources are useful and required to support high-ability learners in the ways outlined in the preceding sections of the policy. Including links to organizations and teaching resources' websites can be helpful.

146

Monitoring and evaluation

Identify the ways in which the success of the program will occur. What mechanisms will you use? What will be the frequency, and how will you communicate successes and areas for improvements?

Schools will have their own templates for developing policies, guided by their relevant educational authority. The process above provides one way of reaching a shared understanding of the 'what, why, and how' of Gifted Education in your school and documenting in a way that is accessible and explicit.

Summary

This chapter discussed various ways that collaboration with schools, organizations, and community partners can be used to enhance and enrich the educational experiences that can be offered to high-ability students. Even though it may feel at times the load of planning and implementing falls to just one person in a school, we can (and I think should) pool our collective resources (time and ideas) to bring these opportunities to life.

A process for developing a Gifted Education policy, bringing together the understandings conveyed in this book, was provided, along with an example.

Chapter Reflection

1. Identify potential partnerships and links within your existing curriculum or programs currently offered in your school
2. Identify ways of collaborating with colleagues in schools
3. Complete planning proforma for mentoring program (if appropriate)

Notes

1 Department of Education and Training. (2018). *Leading Communities of Practice: Roles and responsibilities.* Department of Education and Training. https://www.academy.vic.gov.au/sites/default/files/2019-03/Leading-Communities-of-Practice-Roles-and-Responsibilities.pdf

2 Wenger, E. C., & Snyder, W. M. (2000). Communities of practice: The organizational frontier. *Harvard Business Review, 78*(1), 139–146.

3 de Carvalho-Filho, M. A., Tio, R. A., & Steinert, Y. (2020). Twelve tips for implementing a community of practice for faculty development. *Medical Teacher*, *42*(2), 143–149.

4 Davidson Institute for Talent Development. (2006). *Mentoring guidebook*. Davidson Institute for Talent Development. https://www.davidsongifted.org/wp-content/uploads/2021/03/Davidson_Guidebook_Mentoring_2021.pdf

5 Senge, P. M. (1994). *The fifth discipline fieldbook: Strategies and tools for building a learning organization*. Currency.

APPENDIX E: SAMPLE POLICY

Hogwarts Primary School
Gifted and Talented Education Policy

1. Shared Vision

At Hogwarts Primary School (HPS), we strive to provide a Gifted Education program that is student centred, where strengths are identified and passions enabled to ensure that learning is personalized. We aim to provide flexible and fluid learning environments that allow opportunities for like-minded students to work together on creative and innovative learning experiences that extend beyond the classroom. Teachers, in their role as facilitator, will feel confident in their knowledge and skills in catering for these students and supported through a whole-school approach and access to additional guidance through mentors and support staff. Teachers will, individually and collectively, assume accountability for ensuring these students progress in their learning. Interactions with the wider community, including local secondary schools, and exploiting resources such a parent expertise and mentor programs (such as Scientists in Schools) will provide additional opportunities for lateral learning and for students to feel a sense of purpose and high levels of engagement.

2. Rationale

Gifted Education means ensuring all students are provided with purposeful teaching and learning which caters for personal differences and interests. At HPS, we acknowledge that gifted and talented students are those that achieve or have the potential to achieve in the top ten percent of age peers. All students need to have an opportunity to be extended, challenged, motivated, and inspired in order for growth and self-fulfilment to occur. We recognize that as a learning community we are accountable for meeting the social, emotional, and academic needs of all students to ensure potential is realized. We want HPS to be seen as a leader in education in our community.

3. Definitions

Using Gagné's Differentiating Model of Gifts and Talents, we can define gifted students as those possessing natural ability that places them in the top ten percent of AGE peers. Talented students are those who are achieving in the top ten percent of peers with similar experience. Giftedness can be viewed as the potential to achieve whereas talent denotes achievement. As teachers, our role is to develop and transform natural abilities into talents. This is done through a systematic developmental process whereby students are provided with activities that are appropriate in content, pace, and format for them to develop their skills.

4. Principles and Procedures for Identification

Not all gifted learners are alike, and many underachieve and can go unnoticed in a classroom. This can occur for any number of reasons. It is important that **defensible, consistent identification** measures are in place to appropriately identify all gifted and talented learners. These measures should involve collecting information from multiple sources, including parents. Casting a wide net will ensure that underachieving students are considered. At HPS, the following tools are used to assist in the identification of gifted and talented students:

1. Teacher behaviour checklist
2. Parent checklist for gifted and talented students
3. Achievement scores on standardized assessments
4. Discussions with previous teachers
5. Online aptitude assessment

These measures are undertaken to allow for identification to enable appropriate provision both within and beyond the classroom.

149

5. Staff development program

Staff to be familiar with policy located in the staff handbook. Ongoing professional development in this area will centre in a consistent discussion of programs and sharing of strategies. This will be further enhanced through peer modelling, visiting other schools to share practices, and participating in coaching/mentoring. Catering for gifted and talented learners will form an explicit component of the annual review meeting.

Accessing external professional development for classroom teachers and those involved in any pull-out program provides an additional support.

6. Provision

6.1. Within class

As students spend the majority of time with their classroom teacher, it is essential that a range of within-class programs and strategies are utilized. These include

6.1.1. Differentiated curriculum

Based on knowledge of students (assessment driven) and is student centred. Varying methods of input, process, and output reflecting various learning styles are used. The nature of the work is adjusted, not the volume, as knowledge is extended.

6.1.2. Teaching and learning activities

Teaching and learning activities are organic, responding to the dynamics of the learner. Quality of work is valued over quantity as students are provided with authentic learning tasks. Acceleration is a key aspect in providing teaching and learning activities as the pace of teaching is increased.

6.1.3. Grouping practices

In-class grouping practices will group like-minded students with similar levels of ability if there is an appropriate number that can work together. In the case of a student with abilities that are well-beyond any student in their current year level/grade, then a referral will be made to the student services team for consideration of grade acceleration in the talent domain.

6.1.4. Contracts/independent projects

To be utilized with clear expectations around the focus, with a balanced approach in application to avoid overuse.

6.1.5. Role of assessment

Assessment to be used to inform practice, it underpins the decisions made about both the content to be taught and how it is to be taught. Pre-testing to be conducted in a timely manner to ensure adequate time for considered planning to occur.

Assessment to occur at three stages of the learning sequence – pre, during, and post – to both measure the effectiveness of teaching and modify accordingly. This will ensure students are working within their zone of proximal development.

6.2. *Activities beyond the classroom*

6.2.1. Specialist Activities

Specialist activities with identified students in their talent domains through the use of a weekly pull-out gifted and talented program include, but are not limited to, Mathematics, Writing, Reading, Science, Italian, Music and Performing Arts.

6.2.2. Mentor Activities

Accessing mentors through organizational programs such as CSIRO STEM Professionals in Schools program, ENGQuest, etc. Utilize parents and the school community for experts that may be able to offer some time.

6.2.3. Collaboration with outside agencies

Outside agencies may be utilized to run short/long-term programs/projects with students. This may include user-pays chess club, book clubs, user-pays robotics, CSIRO, museums, art galleries, local high schools, UNESCO, other schools/teachers.

7. Accelerated progression

Teachers will provide opportunities for students to be accelerated in their area of talent both within the classroom as well as through domain-specific pull-out groups. Cross grading in the talent domain for exceptional students will be facilitated through the Student Services team and involve consultation with staff, principal, parents, and student. Grade skipping will be considered in conjunction with psychologist report, parent, and student support.

8. Organizational Issues

Allocation of a staff member to oversee and manage a database of identified gifted and talented students with connections to the Student Welfare Team, and aligned with teaching and learning beliefs, programs, inquiries, and ongoing professional learning. Spaces to be allocated for pull-out groups, which run on a rotational fortnightly timetable to avoid clashes with specialists and ensure access to all curriculum and extra-curricular activities.

9. Transition and transfer

Early identification of gifted students is optimal. As such, communication with parents and kindergartens regarding commencing Prep students is an important part of identification.

Students who have participated in a pull-out program are to be made known to subsequent teachers so they are aware of ability levels.

Classroom grouping strategies should take into consideration cluster grouping of gifted and talented students to ensure they have an opportunity to work with like minds in their class group where possible.

10. Resources

Resources to be utilized include accessing the wider community for local experts, building relationships with secondary schools, and developing a mentor program, universities, other schools, and associations.

Useful links:
Victorian Association for Gifted and Talented Children (VAGTC)
https://www.vagtc.org.au/
Australian Maths Trust
https://www.amt.edu.au/
Carolyn K. Hoagies' gifted education page.
http://www.hoagiesgifted.com/
Creative Competitions. Odyssey of the mind.
http://www.odysseyofthemind.com/
NSWAGTC. NSW Association for Gifted and Talented Children Inc.
http://www.nswagtc.org.au
Star Portal
https://starportal.edu.au/
Tournament of minds
http://www.tom.edu.au/
University of Cambridge: Nrich
http://nrich.maths.org/public/monthindex.php?year=2004&month=01&
University of New South Wales. GERRIC: Gifted Education Research Resource and Information Centre.
https://education.arts.unsw.edu.au/about-us/gerric/
University of New South Wales.
UNSW Educational Assessment Australia.
http://www.eaa.unsw.edu.au/

11. Monitoring and Evaluation

Ongoing monitoring and evaluation will occur through the following mechanisms:

i. Anecdotal feedback and evaluation from staff, students, and parents examining participation, end product, enthusiasm
ii. Self-assessments
iii. Annual review meeting
iv. Online survey (e.g., Survey Monkey)
v. PLT logs to help with planning.

Review: XXXX

Index

Note: Locators in *italics* represent figures and **bold** indicate tables in the text

social general capability 95
socio-economic status (SES) 40
socio-educational advantage (SEA) 85
specialist activities 151
specific learning disorder (SLD) 78, 84;
    sources 84
staff development 146
STEM professionals 140
Sternberg's ACCEL (Active Concerned
    Citizenship and Ethical Leadership)
    model 1, 10–11, **18**, 37, *37*;
    developing leadership 11; exchange-
    based approach 10; target 10–11
student co-created teaching and
    learning 69–70
student mentors 141
student progress, programs and ways of
    communicating **123**
student self-nomination **24**, 35
subject acceleration 56–57
Sustainable Development Goals
    (SDGs) 68
synthesizing information 67

talent 4; development 5–7, 15–16, 94,
    129–130; of students 6
Talent Development Megamodel
    (TDMM) 1, 11–13, **18**; elements
    12; giftedness 11
task commitment 8–9
teacher checklists 39
teacher nomination **23**; form 26, **27–28**

teaching and learning activities 150
teaching strategies 48; access to
    university units 60; curriculum
    compacting 53–56; grade skipping
    57–60; individualized acceleration
    56–57; modifying our lessons 61–65;
    withdrawal programs 60–61
telescoping curriculum **54**
time management 65
Tournament of Minds 125
transactional giftedness 10–11
transformational giftedness 10–11
transition and transfer 146, 152
true peers 104
twice-exceptional learners 38, **66**,
    77–84

underachievement 47, 65–66; factors
    leading to **66**
unhealthy perfectionism 134

verbal academic self-concept 106
volunteering in school 125–126

well-being and learning 94
wisdom and ethics 10
withdrawal or pull-out programs 40–41,
    60–61, 107, 122

year-level-based curriculum 51

zero-tolerance approach 99